Learning Authentic Tango
Mystery Revealed

By Elena Pankey

Title ID: 4914792
Black/ White. No photos
ISBN-13: 978-1500595623
ISBN-10: 1500595624

Contents

Learning Authentic Tango

Dedication

I dedicate this book to my husband Victor, for all his love and generosity. His kindness and patience gave us the chance to walk together through many tango-life lessons to polish and dance it as one.

Prepare to be seduced

***

About the Book

"In the end, it's not going to matter how many breaths you took, but how many moments took your breath away" - Shing Xiong

In this book, readers will explore the most sensual and intimate dance. I will introduce you to a magnificent world of Tango, a magical dance, as I discovered it. In this book you will go through many twists and turns, amazing life stories, about love, failure, passion and success. You will learn how Tango influences, shapes, and impacts the relationships of those who dance it. Furthermore, this book will give you a great insight into the psychology and history of tango, as well as on the communication and forces that revolve around this living dance. You will discover how to better listen to your partner and improve your relationships. You will learn new tango combinations and methods for experimentation and improvisation, while expanding your creativity and spiritual self. You will learn how to be more focused and balanced, how to relax and dance your tensions away. In this book you will find out everything about the leading and following technique, its principles, methods, tricks and meanings. You will discover many new tips and techniques on how to enhance your posture, flexibility and strength, and how to use your creativity, energy and concentration to design your own Tango style. This great guide will help you to improve your dancing and take it to the next level.

***

"In this book, Elena Pankey, experienced dancer and teacher of Authentic Tango, introduces us into the methods and tricks of

the leading and following techniques. She offers us great insight into the key body positions, basic steps and patterns in leading tango, but also into the etiquette, traditions, and correct communication between partners during the Milonga, the famous tango party. While reading it you will learn essential techniques that will transform you in a powerful leader or follower on the dance floor, as well as in your own life. Dancing tango improves brings you more new energy, enhancing your psychological health. This essential book is for men and women, beginners and advanced dancers. It teaches you how to be in control of your own life, while influencing and empowering your partner".
Oana Tarce

***

Elena has compiled a book with her love of the dance shining through each paragraph. She has successfully described all the facts of the dance, and takes people how tango appeared in San Diego. This book is written in an entertaining and effervescent way. It is refreshing and spontaneous like dancing itself. It also responds to Elena's personality. Morwenna Assaf, Middle Eastern Dance Educator and Author

***

It was a wonderful experience working with Elena. She is very kind, generous, and patient. I myself got hooked to her story. I learned amazing stories about Tango people. This is obviously qualifies for a place inside my own memory. Abe Cy

Introduction

Tango is a unique improvisational dance based on communication and the spiritual enjoyment between two people. Tango dancing is both theatrical and eccentric, and depends on the physical and mental cooperation between a man and a woman.

Tango is a beautiful dance of spiritual, nonverbal communication between two people. Tango portrays passion, hate, romance and every other human emotion. It has amusing way to entertain and make your life more enjoyable. It is the most appealing and addictive dance to learn.

Through Elena's stories you will discover people's obsession with the passion of this dance. Tango was born as a dance of singles that were looking for partners to release sexual tension. Tango still remains a dance through which people find romance, and couples get motivated for a better and more exciting life. Tango is not only a fulfilling experience, but it is also an authentic form of therapy.

It depends on the synchronized physical and mental cooperation of a man and a woman, and requires togetherness. When you dance it well, tango brings you joy and countless rewards on different levels of your life and spirit. In tango, people use several forms of movement, such as balancing, turning, moving at a variety of speeds and walking backwards, that are especially favorable to physical and psychological health. It has a lot of great exercises for improving connection between partners. Tango dancing improves your posture, physical strength and flexibility. It increases longevity and it helps release tensions and blockages. Tango is known as well for increasing the hormone levels, like testosterone, and thus making people feel sexier, happier and even less depressed. As it is largely based on the subtle communication between two persons, tango expands your sensitive intelligence, improving the quality of your emotions and developing your abilities to be more present, self-conscious, and to be more empathetic.

Featured as a sensual dance in many popular films, tango allows dancers to improvise as soon as they learn the basic elements. Most teachers first focus on the embrace, and on its special movement, Tango walk. From there on, the dance expands into an infinite variety of combinations and improvisations.

Tango is a special culture, melting pot of people, traditions and cultures. It was borrowed from many nations and many dance elements of many countries. Immigrants from Europe and Africa streamed into the outskirts of Buenos Aires during the 1880's. They looked desperately for a distraction to ease their sense of rootlessness and disenfranchisement as strangers in a strange land. Lonely immigrants and societal outcasts sought to escape from their feelings, but instead they developed music and dance that epitomized them. Tango speaks of frustrated love, fatalism, and of destinies engulfed in pain. For some, it is a dance of a sorrow. Learning the tango philosophy would provide a window into the soul of that special world. The psychology of the Tango is in the poetry of its lyrics, in the music, in the hopes and frustrations, in the illusions and dreams.

Learning Authentic Tango

Tango has musical uniqueness. In any culture all feelings expressed through the music, as well as through dance movements. Tango is a wonderful dance where men personal interpretation of the passionate music creates beautiful movements. Dancing tango means how leader would interpreter the music into the foot patterns. The real tango occurs between the steps, when a person gets ability to adorn. Understanding of the tango music is the first step to identify what steps to dance with this specific music. Moreover, people always energized with the first sounds of Tango music. Some know and recognize their favorite composers or orchestras. Tango gives us an escape from everyday routine and a lot of mental stuff, since most of us, who learn it, is refugees from life. It also discloses the seclusion of some people, and the necessity for the relationship. All of that gives more meaning to their emotions and lives. Those first people, who danced tango in 19 century, had a huge competition, and who fought mostly for the respect. They had nothing in common except the perception of the tango music, and they devised a method of selection: Dance Tango. Learn the Art of Tango persistently, and get delightful pleasure from the learning process. Enjoy yourselves and have the most exciting time on our lessons. Come to study how to be balanced, focused, get positive energy. Investigate how to listen to each other, relax and improve your partnerships. Learn authentic tango combinations, experiment, improvise your tango; dance it while socially having fun. Whatever you do, treat everybody kindly, patiently and forgivingly.

The most valuable, universal meaning of the book some readers might find in the chapter about the really dark side of Tango. The book also describes how the dark energy of the dance moves opportunists forward, as in many other businesses. This dark side of tango most people don't want to see or admit. But it is still there. Having said that, one must add that such dark energy is not a very typical for the dance. Argentine Tango psychology is more complex. This dance is more about sexual tension looking for a release through movements and different partners.

My own story and connection to this place are a good example of how much mystery revolves around the tango world. Tango has not only great bright sides, but it has a lot of deep dark energy in it, too. The next several chapters will be about some tango people, and how tango dramatically influenced and changed their lives.

Keep Looking into my Eyes

All who love tango have their own tango stories. I came into this world because of tango. My mother met my father on the dance floor of a small town from the Russian coast of the Black Sea. My parents loved dancing tango. It gave them passion and fire, and it gave life to me.

Argentine Tango music talks from the heart about the different sides of love and life. It's a music that constantly changes, moving up and down, as we do ourselves in our real life. My parents did not stay together for a long time, and my mother did not live a long life. Tango came to me in waves, in several different periods of my life. Only now, when I look back, I can connect all these small separate pieces into the bigger picture and understand that it was tango that chose me.

My first memory of tango music is from a very long time, when my grandfather, Mina, brought a bandoneon at home. It was a strange big instrument that looked like an accordion and a concertina. I remember him trying to teach me how to play it: You need to open it widely and take all the air in. It will play music, only if you know which buttons to push. And remember, the same button can play different sounds! This instrument will teach you something about magic.

Later on, my parents pushed me to go to a music school, and care with me a huge accordion for 2 blocks. It gave me a lot of frustrations, and ended up soon and unsuccessfully.

When I was about ten years old, I attended a Young Pioneers Summer Camp. During the evenings, adults would gather around the dance floor, and on some days, children were allowed to join them. Tango was a very fashionable dance at that time.

One night the crowd was particularly noisy, reacting very strongly to what was happening on the dance floor. Allured by that din, I also tried to come closer, curious to see what was going on, but I saw just some crazy and strange leg movements, which were doing different tricks under the exciting and passionate music.

Finally, I could look up and was overwhelmed by the intimate and very close position of the ma man and the woman. The couple looked disgustingly sexy. The contrast between the stillness of their upper bodies and energetic leg movements was so strong, that it shocked me. From then on, the couple had my utter and complete attention, being spellbound by their dance. Their heads were slightly turned to the side like they were watching someone inside their embrace. Someone was between them, someone whom they tried to impress, to compete with or seduce. Towards the end of the dance, the man placed the woman on his bent leg and posed for an instance. On the last beat, with the last chord of music, he suddenly looked directly into her eyes. It felt like dream and love hypnotized everybody. It was a moment overflown with a mesmerizing silence. Then the whole crowd exploded and yelled. The man and the woman walked away from the dance floor, fading away...

The next evening, the orchestra started the Tango. I was invited by a boy. In the anticipation of the dance, I forgot about the whole world. I was certain that it was not difficult, and I could dance as I saw the woman dancing the day before. He gave me his hand and Tango came into my soul for the first time. I moved with a boy and the music, and kept on thinking: Keep looking into my eyes...

However, for almost 40 years I did not have any more connections to Tango, and did not have a chance to learn or dance it for a very long time. My next tango experience happened in California while I was watching a performance of one well acclaimed show from Argentina. It made a great impression on me, and after that I tried to see every show they would bring to California. During the intermission, I found some invitations for the dance lessons. It took only that moment's impulse for me to start taking further my newly discovered passion: the tango dancing. So during the next years, I had several trainings with some of the greatest Tango Masters from around the world. One evening, while we were cruising to Alaska, we saw a show by well-known tango-gouaches company. Their performance was mind blowing, and we instantly fell in love with their lyrical and intimate Argentine Tango. I wanted to dance on stage like they did. The second day we went to their tango class, wanting to learn their choreography and perform in their show.

I went directly to them and asked about it. Surprisingly, they all agreed cheerfully. Later, I learn that they all started their dance careers when they were just children and were trained by the best Tango Masters. They have been touring extensively through Asia, Europe and the United States, teaching, dancing, and performing. So during the next 10 days of our cruise, and for several hours a day, we went through an intensive training with the great dancers. My husband, Victor, was recording each lesson, so that we would watch and practice every move later in the cabin.

Learning Authentic Tango

The dancers could hardly speak any English, and I barely understood Spanish. But that was no problem, as Victor became our translator as well. Moreover, for me, their tango language was crystal clear from day one. That 10 day training on the ocean was pure Tango madness, and very hard work. I was feeling so lucky and happy to learn all my new tango tricks with the fabulous leaders, sexy, passionate and extremely skillful men. One of them became and remained my favorite teacher for the following years. At the end of the cruise, I achieved my goal, and learned several fantastic choreographies with our new friends. Also, they kept their promise and casted me on their show. It was an absolute triumph. The cruise ship's huge theater was filled with people, and at the end they all acclaimed it in a long standing ovation. However, that experience became like a high to me. After that, I could not imagine my life without dancing Tango on the stage and without dancing with this energetic group anymore. So we developed a long lasting friendship, and joined them on several cruise ships during the next years. I occasionally performed with them, shining and thriving on that passion of a special dance with skillful dancers. Later, we went to Argentine to polish my tango skills.

People say "what goes around comes around". Life has definitely made one turn for me. In 2004, I was invited to give my Tango lessons right before the show of another well-known Tango Passion performing company. Afterwards, in order to offer more freedom to all dancers, I opened my own school, Tango Caminito School, where I've been teaching special tango techniques that focus on communication, energy and connection.

Dark Energy of Tango

A long time ago, while on a ship in the Black Sea of Russia, I skeptically went to watch a show. Suddenly, I found myself present in the midst of the sounds of a strong passionate piece of music. A tall, skinny young man in a black suit came out on the stage. Then a blond woman with smart blue eyes came out like a cat. She was taller than him, and looked stronger. When they began to dance, everything around disappeared and their mesmerizing energetic tango filled the whole room.

On that evening in the Black Sea, I did not have any plans to move out from Russia. I couldn't imagine myself that one day I would be learning Argentine tango with those two dancers. However, about thirty years later, in San Diego, I was looking for dance lessons and found local tango studio. In the entrée I met a remarkable woman at the front desk. Filled with excitement, I asked: "Maybe you should try a few tango steps with me, while we are waiting for a teacher…"

She confusingly smiled at me and said: "Do you think, you could just simply follow somebody?" Then, she suddenly moved with me, and I was astounded by her strong and accurate lead. This first touch of tango spirit was deeply overwhelming and it was the beginning of our long lasting friendship.

At that dance studio, I quickly noticed that everybody was calling her husband, Our Master. I was curious to know why, but I also got hooked up to the place faster than an eye's blink.

Learning Authentic Tango

The Master was a French Canadian and a ballroom dancer. He had dark eyes and long, colored black hair. He was always wearing a nice suit and tall boots. His English was difficult to understand, but his deep knowledge of Tango was irresistible. And he had another great talent: he knew how to use the power of tango wisely and patiently.

As many others tango students, I kept driving there almost every evening for my many private lessons and practice, getting persistent in my training. Moreover, I attended his "Performance" and "Master" classes, which were designed, as we were all told, for his future teachers. At that time, during the 90s, he was the only tango dancer and teacher in the area. His place also had weekly tango parties, the only one Milonga in San Diego at that time.

However, slowly I noticed that the shadows of the Master's Milonga were filled with spicy intrigues and powerful egos. All these created a very mysterious, intimate and engaging atmosphere there. It was very attractive to many people who were looking for an adventure, and it was a place where many friendships, relationships, and partnerships took shape.

During one of his Milonga, I met another very bright and colorful character, Steve, chef and dancer. His spirit was joyful and energetic, his soul was generous and his enthusiasm was contagious. Steve had the greatest gifts: love for life, people and Tango. Every evening, as his policy, he would dance at least once with a single woman who was sitting alone in the room. It was his joy, and it helped to encourage many others to do the same.

Steve was devoted to Tango for many years. On Saturday mornings, in his tiny kitchen from Orange

County, he cooked delicious food that he would later share with all the people from the Milonga. It was him who brought wonderful cakes for celebrating the dancers' birthdays. We enjoyed sitting at the same table with Steve and his wife Estrella, and take turns in dancing and talking. Steve used to share his philosophy and spirit of Tango with us: "Suppose you bought an expensive bottle of good champagne, perfectly chilled; then you opened the bottle for a drink with a special person. You pop the cork and pour the champagne into a glass filled with shaved ice, and then top it with some tap water. The bubbles are gone, the romance is gone, and the sparkle is gone. You are no longer drinking Champagne. Why would anyone do this same thing with Tango? It is Champagne! It has sparkle! It has bubbles! It is dramatic and stimulating. Use the sparkle and enjoy the feeling and its effect. Tango has a life of its own. Drink Deep and Enjoy!"

I remember one particular spiritual advice that he gave me during one Milonga: "You should dance Tango by using the psychology of the sled dog pack.

There are five lessons to be learned, as a great metaphor for life and tango alike: 1. The lead dog is the only dog that gets a change of scenery.

2. The lead dog always has a pack of yapping hounds at his heels.

3. It is the pack that makes all the noise.

4. They all follow the lead dog's tracks, never making their own, and they never catch up. Now the problem is to make the man leading the sled recognize where he is going (and maybe pat the lead dog on the head once in a while)."

Thee good memory of this bright person will live forever in our hearts.

***

So for many years, the Master's studio managed to exist with the help of his volunteers and supporters. Some were lazy to find another place to learn the dance, and others were simply charmed, or did not have the strength to break the spell of it. Most men were going there allured by the many beautiful single women whom the Master attracted around him, and who gathered there for a Milonga, looking for romance or for some excitement. After all, it was only through the devotion of his students, that the Master's studio became a really successful business with a family-like atmosphere around it.

The Master motivated his many students by telling them that one day they would become tango teachers at his place, a thing which never happened. He kept promising a lot of different things to every one of them just to keep them coming back. The Master had a real canny capacity to make women love tango, and even make them fall in love with him.

One day on an airplane, he talked about tango for hours to a very young Spanish dancer, and invited her to be his student. Soon after, he kicked out his ex-wife, who was his devoted partner for almost forty years, a driving force behind all of his success.

However, all struggles and obstacles made her even stronger. Later we met again at her tiny motor home that she got with the help of her friends. The contrast between her legendary dance past and the modest conditions of her present life was particularly strong. I understood that tango

Learning Authentic Tango

was a way of living, meditation and creativity for her. She had an enormous Tango Spirit in her. As a Slavonic person, I understood her deeply. I could clearly see her roots and felt we had gone through similar trials. Her culture and knowledge made her a unique person with whom one could learn or dance tango.

Time passed. Some wounds healed, and others left deep scars on Anna's heart. But she was blessed with new friends and students. She is teaching Tango as a means to release bad energy, and build fresh energy for a new life. Great Tango Spirit helps us to keep going and maintain our own spirit alive.

Despite all of the Master's ventures, his aficionados kept on supporting and promoting his studio, as he was monopolizing Tango in San Diego. At some point, one of his former students got the strength to overthrow him. She had already learned all his methods of attracting and keeping students. She did not need him any longer, and left his studio along with many of her own followers. As she was looking for independence, she completely separated herself from the Master, opening her own Milonga.

Later, one of the Master's old dreams became a reality and with the money and help of his supporters, he moved to a new location. The new, exotic building was lacking in taste or style, but had a somewhat different spirit. Still there were new tango aficionados who were ready to believe in the Master's promises of being great dancers, teachers, and friends.

In time, tango was becoming more and more commercial everywhere. Some tango teachers found a simple way to make their own name famous by inviting great tango dancers to teach at their place.

Wonderful touring Tangueros came to San Diego and really opened up a great world of tango of new styles and possibilities. Finally, after several other tango instructors visited the city, people realized that there are many other ways to learn and dance.

It is then that the Master got to his well-deserved place: the back room of his studio. On Milonga he "wanted" to dance only with his last Asian wife.

Tango can have a deep power over people's lives. It influences all sides of those who practice it, not only their body, but also their mind and spirit. As it is in other arts and personal development areas, there will be dark Mephistopheles who would use this great energy and power to their own profit. But it won't last long, as Tango has its own way of taking off people's most cherished and relentless masks.

If you are ready to meet new people, see who you really are and let others see you, come and learn the Authentic Tango. You will discover new sides of your own soul, while dancing and going through life changing experiences. Up to the challenge?

***

ENGAGE YOUR MIND INTO SOCIETY'S MOST INTRIGUING AND CONTROVERSIAL DANCE - THE ARGENTINE TANGO

***

Tango is a Walk. Have Love in Your Heart. Dance Joy. Don't Talk. Be Smart, Walk Hard!

***

Enter a Beautiful Magic Universe of Authentic Tango

Magic of Dance

It looks like everything around the culture of tango is interesting. The special theater-like atmosphere of Milonga is enthralling. The creativity and the wide vocabulary of the dance make the learning process a never-ending one. These are only some of the reasons why people can become completely caught up in the world of the tango. Tango makes all sides of human life more inspiring and meaningful. It fills every day with joy and excitement. It enhances concentration and improves physical condition.

On the other hand, tango breeds more thoughts, more feelings, more relationships, more challenges, more puzzles.

Tango is the hug and a meeting dance. It is a game of pure communication between man and woman, where both take the main role. It is not a man-ruled dance, despite the atmosphere. It's a dance created by two. The Argentinean Tango holds a unique place in couple dancing. The body is closer, more intimate than in any other dance form. And yet the legs move faster and with more deadly accuracy than in any other comparable dance. It is this combination of sensual, meditative, relaxed contact in the upper body and swift, almost martial arts-like repartee in the lower body that gives the tango its unique identity. Argentine Tango uses slower music, more of a spot dance, easier to dance on a smaller floor, uses a lot of leg and foot action and the character of the dance is more dramatic. When people dance tango, they often develop a strong relationship during the first 2-3 minutes of the dance.

Sometimes they have their whole lives flashing right before their eyes. Tango can do that to you.

Every couple can be compatible, and move in perfect harmony, or not. On the dance floor, each couple creates their own tango and every time they will perform a different story. When people fail to understand this, they will simply practice the steps without any real emotions or feelings of passion. Many highly skilled women don't like partners who constantly do the same basic steps. Any trained woman needs a new challenge with every new dance partner. When there is nothing new left to discover, the woman will move to another partner. Unfortunately, some men are locked up inside their own prison of several limited ideas, repeating the same steps and patterns on every dance.

These are the types of men who are not interested in variety in their dance, nor in their life. What these men could to do is to think and get more into the character of the music, developing and designing further from there. We all seek something new and interesting, and that is why I don't usually like to predict my leader. Any skilled woman with a high level of tango understanding will be fulfilled only when she is dancing with a skilled leader. But of course, often some disappointments can go together with the pleasure for the sake of it.

Tango with a passionate and connected partner will give a woman the deepest pleasure. The feeling I get when I am in a consonant and sensuous dance I cannot compare with any other pleasure. It comes very seldom and not many couples experience it. But we all try to reach that ideal once we experience it. Only when both dancers are very

Learning Authentic Tango

skillful and capable of a deep connection, can they reach that special pleasure during a tango. That is why this incredible living dance is not for everybody and it doesn't happen with everyone.

In 2005, I met, danced and performed with Maxim Gitano who visited San Diego for a vacation. It was a very exciting and deep tango experience. He was an exceptional dancer, and like a spiritual brother to me. That unique combination of Maxim's sensuality and talent, and my own classical expressions created a very special feeling when we danced. We were both dancing the tango with a strong commitment and awareness, while giving rise to vivid and emotional sceneries. The connection between me and Maxim on the dance floor was above words and meanings. While dancing, we became a sole being moving in perfect harmony on the flow of the sounds, taking Tango to new unexpected heights. All of the above made us unforgettable for those who were lucky enough to watch us dance together. Some people told us that we were sensational on the dance floor. "I was absolutely bowled over your beautiful performance with Gitano. So was everybody else" – said Peggy in her review.

It was my most valuable and memorable experience of authentic tango that I could never repeat again. Our tango story was also documented in some photos which you can see in this book. Some people think that Tango is a personal interpretation of the music. We feel that Tango becomes a dance of magic when both partners are listening and dancing on the same musical instrument at the same time. Our past is only memory. Our future is only illusions and dreams. Our life is now.

Tango gives that awareness of the present moment. Tango teaches how to listen and understand people, and how to be more present and relaxed. It teaches how to keep balance in this dance and life. On the other hand, tango teaches men how to be real leaders, active thinkers, how to react fast, how to empower partners. Men who dance Tango are resourceful creators and authentic initiators. It takes the highest concentration of the mind to be a designer of tango during a Milonga.

In the end, tango is for people who like challenges and are not afraid to try and experience new things. It is for creative people who enjoy learning while dancing.

Tango teaches a follower how to be emphatic and sensitive, and how to surrender.

As such, at the beginning, tango can pose a real challenge for a follower. During the first several years of dancing, many followers might think about how not to miss the lead and to dance on the beats of the music, or how to technically dance it right and make it look beautiful.

It was only after many years of practice that I learned not to think about what to do while I am dancing, and just yield to my partner. When I reach that high level of surrender, I know that I am dancing well. For instance, it is only then that I am able to do adornos without breaking into the leader's space or balance. And it is like a miracle. I feel like flying and melting completely into the music. During such dances, I get that pleasure which I cannot compare to anything else in my life.

It is this great 2-3 minutes of pure emotion during a harmonious, sensitive and sensual tango which really keeps people coming and trying. Although it comes very seldom

Learning Authentic Tango

and not many partners experience it, we all try to reach it. It is only when both dancers are very skillful and capable of deep connection, that they will reach that very special spark during the tango.

All in all, tango for me is not about sex or body; not at all. Tango for me is the space and energy between me and my partner. It is about memories and emotions. It is about the past and the present. It is about freedom and expression.

***

Tango is a Dance of Spiritual Enjoyment, said Carlos Gavito. We dance tango on the beat of the heart"-

***

"Whatever you do in life will be insignificant, but it's very important that you do it" – Gandhi.

Communication of Embrace

At the beginning, Tango was a way of communication for people experiencing the lonely life of immigrants. It still is a way of silent dance communication. Authentic tango has specific features that came about as a result of the way the dance evolved.

Tango was developed in the 19th century by the immigrants and people that were living in the slums and brothels of Buenos Aires and Montevideo. It was born as a combination of many dance elements from different cultures. During that time about 4 million immigrants, mostly men, came to Buenos Aires from many countries looking for work and new opportunities. They were strong, adventurous and courageous people. Some of them were criminals escaping from justice in their homelands. During the day, these portenos were working hard at the docks of Rio de la Plata. They also tried to save some money to go to a brothel or maybe even to a dance hall. They would buy some time there to be with a woman or to dance with her.

It was their way of escaping the loneliness of the immigrant life. And dancing during the evenings would provide them the beautiful illusion of love for a moment. Most of those men were heavy, awkward and stepped down with energy. Their heavy steps gave one characteristic to authentic tango: a special walk with the energy to the floor. Furthermore, these dockworkers from Buenos Aires and Montevideo were poor and could not afford to buy new shoes. So the soles of their shoes would often have holes. In order to hide these holes from the audience, they would keep their feet completely down. This is why in authentic tango one should try always to keep his heels perpendicular to the floor.

At the historical beginning of this dance, men could hardly express deep emotional feelings to the unknown woman with whom they would dance. But they would caress the floor, slide and play with it instead. The best dancers still rarely lift their feet, and when they do, it's only when they want to express a particular move or pose. Most of these first tango men were looking for an embrace, for the consolation or the comfort they would get through the dance.

But there were not enough women, and most of them were pricey and picky. Men had to become very good at dancing in order to get their chance at a dance. Before entering the expensive brothels or dance halls, men tried to improve their skills, exchanging their national dance elements while practicing them on the streets. For example, Europeans brought from fencing two of the most basic movements in tango: corte and parada. And it's so that tango was born from several dance elements of different countries.

This dance revolved around the woman: it was for her and about her. So women were dancing the tango with a somewhat distance and condescension towards men. Moreover, through their embrace, men would try to protect and even hide their partner from the others during the dance.

Women would even look over the man's left shoulder, giving him a signal if somebody approached from behind. This still is the etiquette of Milonga. These particular relationships that developed during their dancing led to the special embrace that gives tango the authentic look: the dancers' feet are far apart, and their upper bodies are close.

During those times, dancing provided a space for real challenges. The competitions between men often led to fights. While dancing, they would hold tight their women with the right arm. Their left arm was always available for handling a knife. This left arm was not important for the dance and a woman never relied on it. Since they danced without having a predetermined pattern (like we still do now), the women were being led by following the chest of their partner.

At the beginnings of the dance, a little orchestra tried to accommodate, please and help people move with the music. Two or three very skilled musicians would accompany the movements of these first couples.

Musicians needed to be smart and fast in order to improvise. Their music was inspired by how the dancers moved their legs. And this is one of the reasons why tango music is still changing all the time.

It expresses on sounds the life story of the dancers. Unfortunately, those first pieces of tango music were not written down, although there must have been also some masterpieces. It was only later that the record companies started bringing to the public the echoes of the original versions of the music. Tango slowly developed into the present form, as did the music. It is still a living form of dance. It continues to develop further by borrowing elements from the modern world and culture.

It was only much later that the dance took a specific form and became more elegant and sophisticated: with extensions in the knees and the body, and with some light relaxation between the steps. Only a hundred years later, after it achieved success in Paris, tango became acceptable in the middle classes of Argentina, and men can now take their wives out at dance halls on Wednesdays night. Tango is not a destination, it does not require running from one corner to another. It is mostly about awareness of the present moment, about your balance, about the sources of your feelings and energy.

Gentlemen, make your partner dance with the music and let her feel the silence through your subtle control of your own thoughts and moves. That will lead to some of your best achievements in dance.

Carlos Gavito once said during a lesson: "Tango is an Embrace. The tango is a way of walking in an Embrace with another person, always looking to the steps together, understanding each other and connecting. Tango is two people who walk as one".

The embrace is what makes tango genuine. At the "Tango Festival" in Buenos Aries, the authentic embrace is the central thing to be achieved. It's through the embrace that the man carries the woman around the dance floor. And the woman dances around the man in the space he provides for her by this frame. Furthermore, the energy inside the tango frame and the relationship inside the embrace are the main attractions for many dancers who come to Milonga. Before you start to dance, take a deep breath and stretch yourself up: put your shoulders back and down, and your ribs up and forward. This is the first thing you need to do. And in this stretched up position you don't move: you just take the air in and the energy from the universe. You listen to the music. You exhale and relax on the next beat. This type of breathing, stretching and relaxing should be part of your dance.

You do it simultaneously with your partner. This is what creates that wave of the two bodies which nobody sees. Tango has this Bandoneon effect or wave effect: when you dance together with your partner you open, and then close. The main source of energy is located under your belly button where your energetic center lays, your tan t'ien. Get your ribs up and inhale. Body stretched up. Keep it open, don't collapse. Try to learn the special terminology and read about what it means. Discovering the history of tango, vocabulary and music will bring you further into this wonderful world that people call the Tango subculture. And have fun while unlocking the tango mysteries.

History of Authentic Tango

Tango is magic. It is passionate, sultry and provocative. Born in the shadowy dance halls and brothels of Buenos Aires in the middle of 19 century, the Tango seduces all who listen and watch.

The Argentinean Tango, a ritual of pleasure and sensuality, holds a unique place in couple dancing. The body is closer, more intimate than in any other dance form. And yet the legs move faster and with more deadly accuracy than in any other comparable dance. It is this combination of sensual, meditative, relaxed contact in the upper body and swift, almost martial arts-like repartee in the lower body that gives the tango its unique identity.

The origin of the word Tango is somewhat obscure. It may have derived from the Tango Andaluz (Andalusian Tango), closely related to flamenco, which was popular in Argentina in mid Nineteenth Century. Beyond the name, there seems to be little to correlate Tango Argentino to Tango Andaluz. African slaves in Argentina had brought with them the rhythmic patterns of the candombe and later black Cubans brought the habanera to Buenos Aires.

A new dance evolved based on the steps of the candombe, the habanera, together with the polka and the mazurka and became known at the time as a milonga (as a dance and a dance hall). Before long, this new dance had been taken up by the new European immigrants and the tango as we now know it was born. If you add kicks and flicks of the legs (some footwork of African dance) to the simple walks and turns of European folk dance and a close embrace that may have originated in the brothels, you have the basic vocabulary of the tango.

Small improvising bands, usually guitar, violin and flute, accompanied the early tangos. Add to this vibrant mix the music - melancholy, ecstatic, growling, predatory, soaring, seeking, heartbreakingly beautiful (especially compared to the insipid kitsch that most ballroom dancing music has become) - and you have the ingredients for something more than a craze. The history of tango starts in 1870, when, in the suburbs of Buenos Aires, dances and songs of different origins came together.

At the very beginning, Tango was danced by men, and probably in brothels. It took a long time until it entered the patios of the conventillos, and even longer still to enter the houses of middle class families. The first tangos were probably played in several places at the same time. The musicians played them in brothels or in academies, which were dancing halls, where people gathered to dance. But although the tango had originated in brothels and in semi-criminal environments with musicians like the Negro Casimiro or the Mulatto Sinforoso, slowly it began to leave the suburb.

Many youths of well off families started going to these outlying neighborhoods where they spent a grand time in brothels. There they also had the chance of picking a quarrel, because for them quarreling could also be fun. Here they learnt to dance the tango. Some of these youths danced the tango in Paris where it immediately generated a frenzy of enthusiasm in the years 1913 - 14. This exotic and sensual dance which provided an excuse for close contact with a single partner was immediately adopted by

Learning Authentic Tango

the Parisians, who transformed it into an overpowering craze.

Everything was tango in Paris: the tango fashion introduced a new skirt with a long slit designed by the couturiers to facilitate the step; yellowish orange became the tango color, tango tea parties were staged in hotels and other gathering places to teach the new dance.

Then, Italy, Germany, England did not want to lag behind and they quickly adopted the fashion. Argentine teachers inaugurated academies all over Europe and in 1914 they took the tango to the United States.

But in spite of the frenzy there were many detractors who criticized tango to be a wild and sensual dance. Even the German Kaiser forbade his officials to dance tango while they were in uniform.

In Paris a countess asked scandalized if it wouldn't be better to be in bed to dance tango.

After the success in Paris, the tango returns to Argentina and becomes socially accepted.

The Orchestia tipica, (typical orchestra, formed by a violin, a piano and a bandoneon), moves from the brothel to the cabaret in the center of Buenos Aires. Their merit has been to have helped the tango gain a firm foothold and to have spread its popularity all over Europe and America.

Around 1910, the bandoneon (a larger, more expressive version of the accordion (probably it was brought from Germany) became the key instrument and identifiable sound of the tango.

In 1920 the tango, which had been spirited and lively at the beginning, became intensely melancholic. The musicians, most of them of Italian origin who had enjoyed musical education, introduced their own nostalgia and loneliness in the tango.

In the twenties, in Buenos Aires, classically trained musicians, such as Julio de Caro, who formed one of the earliest tango sextets, started to take the tango into new areas of subtlety and complexity. The improvising abilities of individual musicians were now held within a more formal musical framework. In the 20s, Rodolfo Valentino had danced tango in his films dressed in gaucho's garments.

In the 30s the orchestras are larger and their interpreters gain popularity through the radio and gramophone records. It is the time of Juan de Dios Filiberto and Juan D'Arienzo. Their tangos are more cheerful and they play in packed ballrooms. The tango has become massively successful. In the thirties (in effect, the swing era of tango) came the first big band sounds. Juan D'Arienzo (the King of Rhythm) and Anibal Troilo created full orchestrated versions of such tunes as La Cumparsita, that became internationally recognizable tangos.

In the aftermath of World War II, under the Peronist government, Argentina started to become politically isolated from the rest of the world. Several decades followed in which the tango developed under a series of political crises. Osvaldo Pugliese, one of the great band leaders of this period, was one of many who were blacklisted or imprisoned for their beliefs.

In 1950 the vanguard led by Astor Piazzolla, Atilio Stampone and Horacio Salgan started plying their new music. The big orchestras are replaced by more reduced groups and the musicians begin to give tango concerts. It is the era of the excellent soloists. By the sixties, rock-n-roll had eclipsed all other popular music world-wide, and then Argentina fell to a military dictatorship. But despite of the law of forbidding groups of more than three to gather together, the tango did not die.

By the eighties (partly under the influence of the great dance teachers, Antonio Todaro and Pepito Avellaneda), the tango had been revived as a form for the stage.

Audiences around the world (through such shows as Tango Argentino) started to become familiar with the musical vocabulary of the tango, and with a theatricalized version of the dance.

To dance tango on stage the couple moved further apart, and the moves became more athletic, and spectacular. A split developed between the stage style, and the milonguero (close-hold) style danced in the clubs and dance halls of Buenos-Aires by people for whom tango was a way of life.

In 1985 a very successful show is performed in Broadway: Tango Argentino by Claudio Segovia and Hector Orezzoli. This production was staged in the entire world and it started a new tango fashion, which became more refined and sophisticated.

It was the second time that the tango became a craze in the United State.

The tango is danced in the entire world today, from Japan to the United States, from northern Europe to Buenos Aires. And thanks to Astor Piazzolla, the tango has been introduced in the concert halls. The Kronos Quartet, Mstislav Rostropovich, Daniel Barenboim, Yo Yo Ma, Gidon Kremer usually include Tango in their repertoire.

In Buenos Aires there has been a rebirth of tango. Tango Volver is the national anthem of Argentina. The 11th December (Gardel's birthday) has been declared the National Day of Tango.

Today by watching it we will research the unique role of the tango in the national landscape, exploring the machismo and passion that feed the dance. We will experience the creativity and sensual inspiration and the passionate feelings that feed this most striking of popular art forms.

First Dancers

At the very beginning, Tango was danced by men. The compadre, the compadrito and the malevo are the three most important male archetypes of tango and were the first to dance it. The compadre was a kind of urban gaucho feared and envied but who had earned respect and a feeling of admiration by authority and courage. He could be a cart driver, a butcher, a tamer or some politician's bodyguard. He always honored the given word and did not doubt to draw his knife when his honor was at stake. A very independent and proud, he was dressed in black with a scarf around his neck and a vicuna shawl on his shoulder. The compadrito was the imitator of the compadre but without his virtues. Although he was always willing to raw his knife because of a sidelong glance, he was fearful of his personal security. He spent his life making a show of his conquests and boasting about his fake temerity. He was also dressed in black with a silken scarf but the jacket and the trousers were not necessarily made of the same cloth. The jacket was short with high shoulder pads and he carried it unbuttoned to be able to take the knife out of the armhole of his waistcoat. His boots were high heeled and his grey hat had a black ribbon, and to crown so much elegance he had a butt or a toothpick in his mouth. In this gallery, the malevo was at the end of the scale. He was a tricky coward, insolent and rude; the malevo felt a deep-seated resentment against society *(Monica Gloria Hoss de le Comte).*

Women's Dream Dance

All women dream to dance with a good, strong leader, who can take them to unknown patterns, to some great heights and to new achievements in their tango ventures. Women like to investigate tango steps with new partners. They like to try new things and face new challenges. The better the leader is, the better the follower is and looks on the dance floor. This is why some followers avoid dancing with beginners. But followers cannot make up a dance for a man, if he does not lead it.

Actually, if we talk about techniques, there are no "man only" or "woman only" techniques. The tango dance is skillful when the man and the woman exchange leads. But they always use the same tango principles and the techniques are the same for both parts. Most women, consciously or subconsciously, feel the need of leaders in their lives. Even when they feel this, they still try to take the burden on their shoulders.

They are so accustomed to teach, talk and help, that they cannot stop doing these even during a perfectly good dance lesson with a great leader. Ladies! Keep your thighs together. Your upper body and shoulders stay with your partner, creating the tango relationship. You always follow the leader's upper body (or shoulders at the beginning). When a leader stops all movement, a woman's belly button should point at his. Keep your own balance and an equal distance between you and the leader. Whatever you do, bring one foot to the other (collect your ankles), or brush them before moving to any direction. Remember that one leg does most of the movement behind the thigh or the knee of the other leg. It is always rewarding to make your partner feel good, and dance with him wherever he is leading you. Followers need to respond with movements based on the messages the leaders send. This is the fun of dancing the tango. But don't anticipate or guess the man's movements, and don't try to do more than he leads or asks. Try not to talk/teach/lead. Listen attentively to the man's lead, and try not to send him your overwhelming energy. Be gentle and surrender tenderly.

Most women need to train themselves not to talk to a man during the lesson or practice. So learn how to listen. Make an effort to silently feel the energy that he is projecting into the frame of the embrace. Give your partner the chance to express himself. Give him a moment on the dance floor to do something on his own. Let him take the initiative!

Modern women are strong, and most of them like to lead. However, in tango, as well as in life, there cannot be two leaders. Learn the leader's part and dance as a leader, if you want to lead. If you want to be a pleasing follower, do whatever your partner asks, even though it might seem wrong. If in the end it does not feel good, you don't have to dance with him anymore.

At the beginning, most of us try to memorize the patterns. But this isn't the right way to follow. Every pattern can be broken and can lead to something unexpected. Every pattern has many windows that are wide open to dancers in search of great pleasure and new discoveries.

Psychology of Elegance

During my years of learning, performing and teaching tango, I discovered several things that I would like to share with you. First of all, every couple dances its own tango. The dance is influenced by the dancer's life experience, personality and own way of thinking, feeling and acting. Moreover, every dance is determined by the performers' abilities to break with the common patterns and to create their own performance. When you dance tango well enough, you will go out of the established design and feel the many possibilities in the most basic steps.

Many people love tango, because they can grow into it. They all keep on coming with different purposes and for different reasons. Most of them keep on dancing because it releases their tensions and anxieties. They go to Milonga because they enjoy the music, love new challenges or feel like creating a new dance. Others go to escape loneliness, to meet new people or just find somebody to communicate with. For the latter, it is very important that the dance makes them feel good, as they forget their everyday worries. People who have a taste for tango will never stop dancing it. Some will find friends or even build their family in the tango community. Whether it is because of the creativity, the music or the exercise on the mind and the body, tango can definitely hook people up. With this in mind, we can look further inside the tango embrace to understand what kind of psychology revolves around this dance floor.

Some lonely people and unhappy couples come to dance tango regularly, running after the illusion of love which they get during the tango embrace. They dance in order to feel something special at least for a moment, something they don't have in their real lives. This can be another side of tango that keeps many people coming to Milonga. However, dancing can be a real form of therapy that could lead to a better way of thinking and living. It can be a way of releasing negative energy and creating a new fresh stream of life. In tango, movements have particular forms of energy. Although, this energy varies from step to step, it is determined by the music, and most importantly by the personality of the dancer. That is why tango can tell us many things about the psychology of the dancers.

If a man grows up in a very controlling or overprotective family, he might acquire too much feminine energy. In this case, his tango will be weak. He will not have any energy in his steps. Lacking initiative, the man will not make any efforts to build energy into his steps, as he does not know when or how to do it. The Feminist movements of the 60s and 70s helped to diminish the energy and initiative of men as well. So now there are plenty of emasculated men who will follow a woman's strong personality in their life and tango alike. These men will constantly carry a fear of not being wrong or not getting the approval from the woman. These types of men try hard to be polite, agreeable and please women. On the dance floor, this will only make them look like cooked potatoes.

In turn, when a woman has too much male energy or too many disappointments and frustrations, she will expresses it through strong, almost aggressive dancing. In such cases, she might take the man's space and energy and even paralyze his will or ability to create. When she is not conscious of what she is doing, she will try to make up a dance for the man.

Nevertheless, most women still desire and dream to dance with a strong leader who has the initiative and the power to take them on an unexpected journey. As such, men and women need to learn how to balance their excess or lack of male energy. This will help them to improve their tango, as well as to live a more harmonious life. So ladies, let the man lead you, and do not talk to him while you are learning or dancing. It is not wise to try to "help" even worth to teach him. Get your pleasure from letting him just be there with you for the moment. One day you might dance with a very skilled leader and then you could be very surprised when you would realize how little you know too. Moreover, one of the greatest things about tango is not knowing what comes next, and just creating movements based on the message your partner sends you. The bigger the circle of your knowledge, techniques and skills, the more opportunities you have to improvise, discover and create new patterns. We all know that tango music is the main conductor of the dance. One of the most challenging things for any dance couple is to be in harmony with each other and to move on the same musical instrument at the same time. But during the first moments of the dance, we might be concentrating on other things. So it is important to listen attentively to the energy inside the tango embrace before you start to dance. In tango, every dancer expresses his/her own life story. Tango opens up your character while you dance it. Your tango will show whether you want it or not, who you really are at this present moment of your life. Nobody will ever be able to hide any thoughts or feelings during the dance. For instance, if you like to fight, your dance will show it, as it will be more shaky than smooth. If your thoughts are chaotic, your dance will have abrupt movements out of harmony.

On the other hand, if you are thoughtful and loving, your dance will be attentive, courteous and tender.

If you have any passions or sadness in your life, they will be expressed in your tango as well. Tango brings people together, but it can separate them. It has some mystery and magic in it. You will clearly recognize the healing benefits of the dance, once you put your own consciousness into it. Then you can purposefully improve the health of your body, mind and spirit.

It is clear, that for the elegant and beautiful tango, everybody should learn and use the correct techniques. Moreover, in life and dance alike, everybody needs to develop the ability to listen to the partner, and dance some embellishments between the steps. While dancing most of us willingly or not will tell our own life stories. So what is your tango story?

Basic Rules for Followers

1. Listen carefully to your partner. Don't teach him anything even though you might think you know more.

2. Don't talk to him during the lesson or practice. Don't try to help him by telling him how he needs to do the steps.

3. Try to please him and support his efforts of learning with you.

4. Feel and be willing to go with your partner wherever he takes you on the dance floor.

5. Close your eyes and read the energy that comes from inside.

6. Learn the correct tango techniques.

7. Listen to the music while moving with your partner. Don't assume what comes next.

8. Learn patterns, but be ready for your leader to break them. Don't follow some fashion without thinking, without adjusting tango style to your body-mind.

Follower's Head position

For those who learned about the history of the tango movements, it is obvious that everything that we dance has psychological and sociological meaning. When you dance with a man, you choose what to dance and think about the meaning of the steps. So it is good to remember a short historical note before coming to the tango lessons:

1. Lady's head is looking over the man's right shoulder. This is a position recommended only when both partners are of the same height. And despite appearances, this position is not a sign of a close embrace. Meaning: the

lady does not care about her partner, does not want to face him, does not have anything in common with him, does not want to be involved emotionally with him, and might be even looking to somebody else behind him.

2. Lady's head is looking over the man's left shoulder (a window of dreams). Her chin is up and parallel to the floor. This position is used for any heights of the partners. Meaning: It's a friendly and polite way to welcome communication. The lady's head position is saying: "I don't care about other men right now. I am with you to investigate 3 minutes of this music. We could go together in one and the same direction, as a union". All in all, the position of the head is the personal choice of the woman, as it is the close or open embrace.

If a woman does not want to be intimate with her partner during the dance, she chooses an open embrace. She chooses the distance between her and her leader. The man could not force her otherwise, or insist on a tight hug. It is always a woman's choice. Some people who want to experiment with the movements, but are waiting for somebody else, will dance in an open embrace. Moreover, for skilled dancers, the open/close embrace will be changed all the time during the dance.

Some movements require more close embraces, and others should be danced in an open embrace. In any case, this is a very technical question which should be well researched by any student or dancer.

Moving Meditation

Some people feel that tango is a moving meditation. Others feel that tango is a relationship therapist. Through the harmony of connected movements, we learn how to improve relationship and marriages, and enhance the power of passion and love. But some people are afraid to learn the Argentine style of tango, and others will just quit after several lessons. This happens primarily because of the fear they feel when they realize that they cannot hide anything from their partner while dancing. They cannot hide their attitude, intentions, or inner feelings. Tango will take off all your masks and reveal your real face.

Furthermore, it is always useful to learn both parts in order to be aware of what your partner is doing at all times. The unique design of tango lessons improves both partners' ability to communicate with each other, read and exchange the energy inside the tango frame, and use that energy in order to become sensuous dancers. It is necessary to learn how to listen to each other, while developing a strong frame, balance and positive energy. The character of tango is given by the combination of legato (smoothly connected) and staccato (disconnected) musical phases. You have to feel when and where to be light, to float along the floor or ground yourself. Every step is in a relationship with the previous and the next one. Identify these while learning tango. Furthermore, you have to be aware all the time where your arms, hips, thighs and feet are. You need to make sure that all parts of your body are in each and every movement of your dance. It takes a special effort before it would become an automatic process. It is the fluid and thoughtful transitions that make this dance complete. All tricks and steps, poses and figures should have the glue that holds everything together: the transitions from one movement to another. Learn and use special transitions to create texture and melody within the dance. The music is changing all the time. Listen to it first. Try to dance this changing music. Keep up your energy and the character you are portraying during every transition. For example, your simple side start could be done as a lead to a Boleo, and then to a Salida. Also, it could be done as a lead to a pose La Punta del Pie. Also, it could be a leading move towards a woman, such as Molinete. It will depend on what you are planning to do before you start to dance. Your mind should move fast, but you shouldn't move without thinking. Tango has a domino effect: if you make sloppy transitions, such as not brushing, not waiting for a woman to finish her move, it will lead to a sloppy ugly dance. Knowing where you are coming from and where you are going to will help a lot. In order to make a strong lead, first take a deep breath in and exhale with your partner on the step. It is important to visualize and send forward your energy out from your chest, head and mostly from your Tan-Dien. This is your first lead. And a sensitive partner will read it in your frame. Try all of the above, and you and your dance will shine.

Tango Music

Tango music has the 8-beat counting System. It is good to practice to the silence and sound of the music, using this 8-beat counting system to organize the movements and connect to the resonance of a variety of musical landscapes.

Timing was crucial for the smooth dancing flow. During the dance, you carefully listen to the changing 8 beats of the music; you see better space and time. The music stimulates your body and you move with the music, improving your strength and flexibility. Take advantage of the heat and apply ability generated from the previous movement.

In order to shine on the dance floor, you have to learn to feel the tango music as well. Specific pieces of music have specific energy types for the dance. It is important to listen to and dance on the music. But the music comes not only from what it is on the CD, but also from what is inside of you.

For Tango dancing we all need to have some sense of rhythm and some musicality to be able to dance any dance. Rhythm means how we use our feet to interpret beats of the music. Each dance has its own rhythm. Syncopations are when a dancer takes 2 steps on 1 beat of music. Also, good rhythm makes an effortless look on the dance floor. The luck of rhythm makes stiff and awkward appearance.

Tempo is the speed in which the music is played. When you are able to count music by using beats and rhythms, to distinguish the syncopations, and to find that down - strong - beat, you will be music, to feel the music, and dance silence in it - silently.

Some beginners dance every beat in tango. It might be OK with staccato music, but there is no necessity for it. When people do it, the dance looks like an exercise.

During milonga music will be presented in Tandas with Cortinas (3 sets with musical interludes). The music is changing all the time. Listen to it first. Try to dance this changing music.

Being a Leader

Gentlemen! I have some news: you have to be leaders in Tango!

Tango is a dance based on two basic roles: the leader, the role usually assigned to the man, and the follower, the role assigned to the woman. Excelling at the art of tango involves not only mastering the leading and the following techniques, but also exchanging these roles during the dance.

Leadership means different things to different people, and different things in different situations. Obviously, leadership is the art of leading.

Recently, I asked my husband, Victor Pankey, who has been dancing Tango for the last 20 years, what is leadership for him in Tango and life.

I got as always his sophisticated, elegant, and so precise answer: "Real leadership is the ability to see the possibilities of the future and visualize a way to get to those possibilities, for the benefit of your followers. Many who are looked up to today as "leaders" are simply opportunists that rise to positions of a power. Some notable exceptions notwithstanding, the ruling elite class is comprised of self-centered egoists competing with each other for ever higher levels of control, all the while protesting their concern for the benefit of the unthinking masses. This is precisely the opposite of leadership required in Tango. Few successful Tango leaders enjoy controlling their partners.

The real satisfaction for a Tango leader comes from providing opportunities for the follower to find joy in movement which, by his leads, he makes possible."

Learning Authentic Tango

Leading is about finding your energetic center and working with it in order to control and lead your partner where you want. Dancing the tango by using these leading techniques teaches you how to better communicate with the people around you, while increasing your balance, concentration and mental power.

Tango now is danced around the world. Elena said, that *Tango is just a walk, with LOVE in your heart.*

It means that a leader, at all times during the dance, needs to think about the comfort of his lady. But it is a two sided coin: the lady needs to listen to the energy impulse that he sends, as a part of his lead, to her.

First, a leader needs to have the vision which steps or patterns would be escorted the follower in the dance. Then, you bring your partner to the result that wouldn't have happened otherwise. If you want to achieve great leadership skills, you need to have inspiration, persuasion and personal connection to the partner. Finally, after some years of persistent dancing, you will get the power and authority to invite any skilled lady to enjoy with you the freedom of real improvisational dance, and the wonderful pleasure of connected tango. It's not just the creation of results that makes good leadership. Good leaders are able to deliberately create challenging results by enlisting the help of his follower. These are some important characteristics of good leaders in tango and in life: You need to develop self-awareness: what is your inner emotional state right before the dance. Turn to the music and then to the energy of your partner; read it.

Before starting the dance, sit for a while quietly and think about what are your strengths, what steps you know well and what will you lead. Learn about your capabilities, and not about your limitations.

1. You need to develop self-direction. Before leading your partner to any combinations, you have to think about several patterns in advance. Then, you are able to direct yourself effectively and powerfully. If you already have learned the techniques and patterns, you know how to get things done, how to organize tasks, and how to avoid procrastination. Also, you need to know how to generate energy for the tanda (3 tangos in a row), and to calm yourself when you get angered. Since any tango lasts only about two to three minutes, you have to learn to make decisions quickly.

2. You need to develop a vision of your dance. It comes in time. You're working towards a goal that's greater than yourself. First, it could be some simple steps that you execute perfectly and in a harmony with a partner.

Later, you would add more new and polished steps to what you know and add them to the music piece. Working towards a greater vision to give more pleasure to your partner is far more inspiring and rewarding than just dancing every time the same combinations. 3. You need to develop ability to motivate your lady to be as pleasant as possible to you during those 2-3 minutes of the shared tango-life in tanda. Leaders don't lead by telling women what they have to dance. Instead, leaders cause partner to want to accommodate him pleasantly. If you care for your partner, you receive more compassion in return. When women sense that you want to please them, they in turn want to please you. A key part of this is cultivating your own desire to give her maximum pleasure. It could be achieved only by your strong, powerful, skilled techniques. Such dancers are also more socially in tune.

4. You need to develop an ability of social awareness. During Milongas it is your knowledge of the etiquette, line of the dance and politeness to others on the dance floor.

Most of these features have direct ties to your emotional intelligence (EQ). Leaders with high EQ are in reality more self-aware. They know their mental processes, how they put steps together, and how to direct themselves according to the music. Leadership is often about hard skills. A leader who understands what drives his dance is more valuable. The leader who can get his lady to perform at her best will get ultimately winning results. He will be always the desired partner for any follower. Leadership is the art of getting your partner to do something you want would be done because she wants to do it. You set the direction, build an inspiring vision inside yourself, and create something new from all your regular steps. The dance of leaders is the dance of an exciting and inspiring Tango. You guide your woman to the right destination in a smooth and efficient way. Your visionary thinking will steadily improve your performance on the dance floor, as well as in your life.

When you began to learn Tango, you will have lots of enthusiasm for it. But soon you would realize that it is a hard world.

It can be difficult to find ways to keep your vision inspiring after the initial enthusiasm fades; leaders recognize that and are ready for it in advance.

The effective leaders will expect that hard work leads to good results. The good results lead to attractive rewards, pleasant dancing, and success in Milongas. This motivates men to work hard to achieve success, because they expect to enjoy rewards. Moreover, whatever you do, your goal should be from the start to become an expert in tango, and get the expert power on the dance floor, as well as in your life. People admire and believe in these leaders because they are expert in what they do. It will bring you the credibility, and the right to ask any woman to dance with you any time you want and follow you well. This makes your life a real joy. Leaders can also motivate and influence other dancers through their natural charisma and appeal. So, you might think how to improve those characteristics, as well.

Tango is a dance that relies on two basic elements made up of two attitudes: a man, who is a leader, and a woman, who is a follower. It is the result of the interaction between these two attitudes combined with the dancers' own interpretation of the music, according to their particular character. Every leader creates his personal tango.

Leading is one of the two basic roles of the tango dance. While usually the man dances in the leading role, and the woman in the following role, when the dancers are both skillful, they will exchange these roles between them frequently.

Leading is essential to any tango dancer, whether he is a beginner, or at an advanced level, a man or a woman. Moreover, the leaders in tango are the real creators of the dance. It's they who initiate the movements and improvise with the dance patterns in order that the dance flows smoothly on the music. But a good leader needs a good follower to make a beautiful dance. Leading techniques have different levels and stages. Although there are several leading techniques, there isn't one for one style.

First, a man turns his upper body or his torso to the direction where he wants a follower to go. The follower responds according to her first rule, following the upper body of the leader.

Although the torso of the leader gives a pivot to the follower, it does not provide an indication for a step yet. Second lead is the lead for a movement: leader changes his body weight from one leg to the other on the spot or during the movement. This weight changing makes the follower change her body weight together with the leaders. The third leading technique is by using the right arm, which should always be parallel to the dance floor. The right arm of a leader moves from the right side of the follower (close embrace) to the left side of the follower (open embrace), depending on the steps. For some movements men use the palm of their right hand to lead their partner to one direction and their fingers to lead the partner back to the opposite direction (as in an ocho for example). Moreover, the leader's left wrist should not be close to the chest and the heart. The wrist should be on a plane halfway between the two bodies, extended comfortably to the left. Whatever you do in tango, your knees are flexed a little. Don't keep your weight on the heels; walk with your toes forward, carefully landing the feet on the floor.

This is your main lead, gentlemen! Your walk forward should look like somebody is holding you from behind and is trying to pull you back, while you are trying to escape.

Basic Rules for Leaders

Take a romantic notion and make it your reality

Leadership means different things to different people, and different things in different situations. Obviously, leadership is the art of leading.

Recently, I asked my husband, Victor, who has been dancing Tango for the last 20 years, what is leadership for him in Tango and life. I got as always a very sophisticated and elegant but so precise answer:

"Real leadership is the ability to see the possibilities of the future and visualize a way to get to those possibilities, for the benefit of your followers.

Many who are looked up to today as "leaders" are simply opportunists that rise to positions of power. Some notable exceptions notwithstanding, the ruling elite class is comprised of self-centered egoists competing with each other for ever higher levels of control, all the while protesting their concern for the benefit of the unthinking masses. This is precisely the opposite of leadership required in Tango.

Few successful Tango leaders enjoy controlling their partners. The real satisfaction for a Tango leader comes from providing opportunities for the follower to find joy in movement which, by his leads, he makes possible."

Tango now is danced around the world. First, you need to have your vision which steps or patterns you would escort your follower to dance. Then, you bring your partner to the result that wouldn't have happened otherwise. If you want to achieve great leadership skills, you need to have inspiration, persuasion and personal connection to the partner. Finally, after some years of persistent dancing, you will get the power and authority to invite any skilled lady to enjoy with you the freedom of real improvisational dance, and the wonderful pleasure of connected tango. It's not just the creation of results that makes good leadership. Good leaders are able to deliberately create challenging results by enlisting the help of his follower. These are some important characteristics of good leaders in tango and in life.

You need to develop self-awareness: what is your inner emotional state right before the dance. Turn to the music and then to the energy of your partner; read it. Before starting the dance, sit for a while quietly and think about what are your strengths, what steps you know well and what will you lead. Learn about your capabilities, and not about your limitations.

1. You need to develop self-direction. Before leading your partner to any combinations, you have to think about several patterns in advance. Then, you are able to direct yourself effectively and powerfully. If you already have learned the techniques and patterns, you know how to get things done, how to organize tasks, and how to avoid procrastination. Also, you need to know how to generate energy for the tanda (3 tangos in a row), and to calm yourself when you get angered. Since any tango lasts only about two to three minutes, you have to learn to make decisions quickly.

2. You need to develop a vision of your dance. It comes in time. You're working towards a goal that's greater than yourself. First, it could be some simple steps that you execute perfectly and in a harmony with a partner. Later,

you would add more new and polished steps to what you know and add them to the music piece.

Working towards a greater vision to give more pleasure to your partner is far more inspiring and rewarding than just dancing every time the same combinations.

3. You need to develop ability to motivate your lady to be as pleasant as possible to you during those 2-3 minutes of the shared tango-life in tanda. Leaders don't lead by telling women what they have to dance. Instead, leaders cause partner to want to accommodate him pleasantly. If you care for your partner, you receive more compassion in return. When women sense that you want to please them, they in turn want to please you. A key part of this is cultivating your own desire to give her maximum pleasure. It could be achieved only by your strong, powerful, skilled techniques. Such dancers are also more socially in tune.

4. You need to develop an ability of social awareness. During Milongas it is your knowledge of the etiquette, line of the dance and politeness to others on the dance floor. Most of these features have direct ties to your emotional intelligence (EQ). Leaders with high EQ are in reality more self-aware. They know their mental processes, how they put steps together, and how to direct themselves according to the music.

Leadership is often about hard skills. A leader who understands what drives his dance is more valuable. The leader who can get his lady to perform at her best will get ultimately winning results. He will be always the desired partner for any follower.

Leadership is the art of getting your partner to do something you want would be done because she wants to do it. You set the direction, build an inspiring vision inside yourself, and create something new from all your regular steps. The dance of leaders is the dance of an exciting and inspiring Tango. You guide your woman to the right destination in a smooth and efficient way. Your visionary thinking will steadily improve your performance on the dance floor, as well as in your life. When you began to learn Tango, you will have lots of enthusiasm for it. But soon you would realize that it is a hard world. It can be difficult to find ways to keep your vision inspiring after the initial enthusiasm fades; leaders recognize that and are ready for it in advance.

The effective leaders will expect that hard work leads to good results. The good results lead to attractive rewards, pleasant dancing, and success in Milongas. This motivates men to work hard to achieve success, because they expect to enjoy rewards.

Moreover, whatever you do, your goal should be from the start to become an expert in tango, and get the expert power on the dance floor, as well as in your life. People admire and believe in these leaders because they are expert in what they do. It will bring you the credibility, and the right to ask any woman to dance with you any time you want and follow you well. This makes your life a real joy.

Leaders can also motivate and influence other dancers through their natural charisma and appeal. So, you might think how to improve those characteristics, as well. For tango dancing we all need to have some sense of rhythm and some musicality to be able to dance any dance. Rhythm means how we use our feet to interpret beats of the music. Each dance has its own rhythm. Syncopations is when a dancer takes 2 steps on 1 beat of music. Also, good rhythm makes an effortless look on the dance floor. The luck of rhythm makes stiff and awkward appearance. Tempo is the speed in which the music is played. When you are able to count music by using beats and rhythms, to distinguish the syncopations, and to find that down - strong - beat, you will be music, to feel the music, and dance silence in it - silently. Some beginners dance every beat in tango. It might be OK with staccato music, but there is no necessity for it. When people do it, the dance looks like an exercise.

1. Dance with a long extension in the leg from the hips down. 2. While stepping forward, extend the legs from inside the thighs. 3. While stepping backward, take long steps from the hips. 4. Don't look at the floor and don't stare at your partner; it is recommended to look to the left for the next space to move to. 5. While walking, place your body off your foot and step on the ball softly; do this like an airplane would land, and try not to step with the heel first. 6. Keep your body centered, from the waist line slightly forward to the partner. 7. Try to dance smoothly as if you were floating; your partner should not feel when you are landing your feet. 8. Left foot lands slightly pointing towards left; right foot lands pointing towards right. 9. Don't bounce up and down. 10. Never move your left arm or hand. Your right arm is the main connection, the main part of your frame and it controls the space where your partner is dancing. Breathe well during the dance, as it will improve your energy lead. And remember: we exhale when we put some effort to push something forward or like when we lift some weights. Men lead by exhale and by

putting their energy into it. Do not freeze your breathing while dancing. When you inhale, take your ribs up and slightly forward and suck your tummy in. Collect the energy from inside. Then push your energy towards your partner, like you want to lead and move her strongly. You want to control her through your own energy and intention: concentrate your energy inside your tummy, around your belly button; push forward before or when you begin to move. Push it in the direction where you want to go. The day when the leader will become truly skillful, he will lead by his belly button, which is stronger, though it is still an invisible control. For any side or back start/step: Stretch your leg, and bring your whole body weight on it. Collect your feet, relax the knees and move to the next step. Remember, your leg goes forward, back, and to the side. Gentlemen, please remember some secrets of all these beautiful tango positions: they lay in your posture and frame. You should never lean forward or backward, but keep your upper body straight up. So don't break your frame, watch your elbows and don't drop them down. Don't lead by moving your elbow. Your elbows should stay in front, and never behind. Keep your arms strong from shoulder to elbow. In order to control a woman, you need to keep your leading right palm and fingers on either side of her back, across her spine. Keep the circle around your partner, and the upper body in contact with her. Don't squeeze her and always wait for her to finish her moves. Be elegant and patient. Make tango poses often and think about new combinations of steps. Create a relationship during the dance, feeling your partner and following the music. It is better not to repeat ochos more than 2 times in a row. Make as many variations as possible, changing your steps and rhythm as often as the music allows it. The leaders are the creators of this dance, but while dancing, they should refrain from verbally explaining to their partners where they need to go or how they should move. Leaders should make the followers understand what they want them to do by communicating through the movement of the torso. If the follower doesn't understand the leader, it means that something is wrong with the leading. So learn how to move the torso correctly, keeping your shoulders and arms as one block.

Key Body Positions
Enjoy your Presence,- your Powerful Now!

Keep your left arm and elbow still in the area between the bodies. Keep it in front of your left side, creating an equilateral triangle with your left side and the floor. Depending on the woman's height, your left arm will go slightly up or down. The follower will push hard on it, otherwise their arm will be like a wet spaghetti. But under any pressure or no pressure, your left arm does not move anywhere.

Your right arm follows the bra line of the woman. It might change positions slightly, depending on the partner's height. However, the arm position is always parallel to the dance floor. Keep your fingers, as well as your palm, in contact with your partner's back. Use your hand to lead the movements, pressing your fingers or the hill of your palm stronger. Your right arm always moves parallel to the dance floor. In a close position, the arm is closer to woman's right side, holding her under the armpit.

For an open position, you move your right arm to the left side of the woman.

Whatever you do, keep the follower's space under your control, and never stretch your right elbow. When moving forward, your left leg is always stretched completely forward (including the knee). You never step or move forward (for example, in a salida) with your left knee bent.

Stretch your left knee for a strong extension between movements, locking it and relaxing it right before each movement. Lead with your head, turning it to the left for her left Molinete or turning it to the right for her right Molinete.

Keep your shoulders down in a relaxed position. While keeping your right shoulder down, keep your right arm far away from your side, in a diagonal position. Never bring your right arm close to your right side.

Keep your rib cage up and forward. Focus on it and don't collapse on it. You can use it to lead women, by pushing it forward.

Turn your hips to the direction you want to move, keeping your torso facing the woman. Dance each movement with high precision.

Feel the music: every 4 beats you change the pattern of the steps. And remember, tango is not a destination. You don't run towards a destination, but dance around your partner and for her. Tango is a dance for the support, balance and pleasure of your partner. You dance to show her off.

Strong Frame

Argentine Tango is a wonderful dance to watch in the shows, when the best dancers present flashy movements. That kind dancing is famously addictive. However, it creates a wrong stereotype, and makes many people to be afraid to actually learn how to dance it right.

However, then only the bravest students would come to the classes because of their curiosity about dancing tango. The first and the most important thing they all need to know is how to embrace and keep the strong frame. It would shorten the learning time, and prepares all students to enjoy Argentine Tango sooner and faster. Knowledge is power. The journey to all of those flashy movements is long and mostly illusions.

On the other hand, it would bring to anyone a lot of good benefits and exercises. Dancing at a high level of intensity will stimulate the heart and lungs. Movements that are done at a varying speed will also help to strengthen the nervous system.

Moreover, for those who want to lose some weight and get well faster, we strongly recommend variations by changing the level of elevation during tango jumps, sentadas, leans and drags or any other movements that include moving up and down from the floor. First, for beginners it is the best to learn Tango De Salon, which is the classical foundation.

Tango De Salon: Position/frame cannot be broken as long as the music plays. The partners must constantly hold each other, allowing only minor elasticity during certain figures. This elasticity should not be used couple's embrace. Certain figures are more appropriate than others when dancing in this style or in a close embrace. Within these guidelines it is possible to perform many of the figures commonly used including barridas, sacadas, and enrosqyue. All of them danced while keeping the feet on the floor. Couples should constantly move counter clockwise around the floor, and avoid remaining in the same place for more than two musical measures. It is very different from the stage Tango.

Stage Tango: Ganchos, leaps, trejadas (climbs) and others big steps that are dangerous for the social environment, and they should be excluded during the dance party, Milonga. My Argentinians friends explained the official rules of the Tango Salon. These rules were used during the Tango World Championship: "Once a couple is formed, the partners shall not separate as long as the music is playing. This means that they cannot break the embrace, which is considered the tango dance position. For the position to be considered correct, the partners must constantly hold each other by means of the embrace. During certain figures this may be flexible, but deviating from the embrace should be not continuing throughout the entire piece. All movements shall be performed within the space allowed by the couple's embrace. The jury will give special relevance to the couple's musicality, elegance, and walking style. Within these guidelines, participants may perform any figure commonly used, including barridas, sacadas close to the floor, and enresques. Couples, as in a real dance hall, shall constantly move counter clockwise and avoid remaining in the same place for more than two musical measures. No contestant may raise his or her legs above the knee line."

It is the most beneficial to learn The Golden Age of Tango. The Golden Age of Tango started in 1935, and the next decade was one of striking creativity in tango. The dance developed into one of the most beautiful couple dances in the world. Composers, arrangers, lyricists and singers all hit united, and each stimulate the other on to ever more stunning achievements. In the late 1940s the music and the dancing began to separate again, as musicians began to play for a bigger audience, concerts, records, radio, which were designed to listen and not to dance. Singers, too, who were becoming stars in films and on records, wanted to be freed of the rhythmic constraints imposed by the requirement to please dancers. For a while the two schools existed side by side. In any style of tango (Authentic or a Nuevo), one of the most important things is to have a strong frame. Leaders can achieve this by not ever moving back/forth their left bent elbow, as well as not moving the hand holding the woman's right hand. A strong frame moves you through the space. Here are a few tips for developing that strong frame: 1. Avoid the effect of a cooked potato. Keep your energy levels high. Your posture should always be in the upright position and the core of your body strong.

2. Watch out for a wet spaghetti effect.

It is difficult to dance together as a team when either the follower or the leader has lifeless arms or soft shoulders.

3. Beware of the palm resistance. When a leader pushes a follower's hand, her hand should respond with the same amount of energy. She has to read what is in the tango

embrace, what the leader is trying to say, and respond accordingly. Enjoy your tango!

Improving Your Techniques

Tango Argentine is a creative, improvisational dance. It is great fun and pleasure when both partners know the correct techniques and share the same level of energy, skills and understanding of the music. During tango lessons, students learn that with the same movements they can do many different things, by feeling the opportunities they get to adorn and enhance. During the lessons, students investigate where the physical touch is, when the energy of the movements have stronger accents, how leaders use the frame to lead their partners, and how followers read the frame to move in harmony with their leaders. Moreover, in order to dance smoothly, it helps if you learn the historical background of the steps, as well. For example, a big boleo might have come from men's fights, as they were trying to clean the space behind them without looking back. The special tango walk with torque was born in Buenos Aires when men were ready to fight to protect their women, while dancing.

Go to lessons persistently and in sequences with the same teacher at least for ten lessons. Then you might see the logical and psychological connections. It is for the best to try to separate your personality from the dance. During the lessons it would be good for you to remove all obstacles between you and your teacher, if you feel you have it. However, you need to have a compatible teacher with the same type of energy.

Learning Authentic Tango

Many tango steps you learn from different teachers might be the same. But the combinations of the steps will be very different. The design of the dance – the order of the steps and how they are brought together to match the specific music – is the responsibility of the leader. It concerns his ability to think fast, be creative and improvise.

Professional tango dancers know all the steps, so they compete in speed, and in creating the best combination for a specific piece of music.

The question now is how fast can you perform and combine steps, more skillfully and more precisely. Moreover, you can learn many different combinations, but if you don't practice them several hours a day, some of them would go away easily.

Furthermore, since your brain is the best computer, try to watch the best tango movies. The computer inside your brain will record the best movements and styles. If you have been learning tango with a smart teacher, video lessons will help you to recognize movements. Watch what other dancers are doing between the steps, what kind of adorns they dance. Personal style comes mostly with adorns that are done well. For example, a woman needs techniques to perform a gancho well. But since gancho is the strongest intimate movement, it is up to the woman whether she does it or not. For women, it is not necessary to do a gancho, even when men clearly invite it.

Men lead, but women decide what to do. She can easily choose to dance a boleo instead. However, if she chooses to do a gancho, she should not lift the upper part of her leg or knee. It is the movement of her leg down and inside, between men's legs. Her knee should point down directly to the floor. Moreover, you can learn many different combinations, but if you don't have somebody to practice with, you will not progress. This is why it would be ideal to find a person with whom you can learn, practice and experiment. When couples go to tango lessons together, they can take their new knowledge home with them.

In order to shine on the dance floor, you have to learn to feel the tango music as well. Specific pieces of music have specific energy types for the dance. It is important to listen to and dance on the music. The music comes not only from what it is on the CD, but also from what is inside of you.

Tango Principles

The thirteen primary principles of Tango are the foundation of the practice and dance. They provide a framework for experiencing fitness as a personal growth during tango learning lessons.

They are the tools you use to get fit, stay healthy and make lifestyle changes. There are special tools to dance elegant tango, even for a social purpose. Take the time to become physically intimate with each principle and your tango practice will soar to new heights!

Principle 1: The Joy of Movement

Joy is the primary sensation to seek from all movement. If you momentarily lose joy, tweak your movement until joy arises again.

Principle 2: Natural Time and the Movement Forms

All of your Tango movements are done in your own personal, natural sense of time, with and according to your interpretation of the tango music.

Principle 3: Music and the 8-beat counting System. Tango music has 8-beats. It is practiced to the silence and sound of music, using this 8-beat counting system to organize the movements and connect to the resonance of a variety of musical landscapes.

Principle 4: Improvisational Tango

It comes only after students have learned some specific combinations, structure and basic steps and the correct techniques to perform them. Then, time will come to break all rules and improvise by using the combinations, creating your own unique tango. Only then, "anything goes"; movement wise. Free dance allows us to let go of structure.

The Free Dance system is an eight-stage movement process that stimulates creativity.

Principle 5: Awareness and Dancing Through Life.

In Tango, as well as in some other forms of moving art, you become aware that every movement in life is a part of your dance, and that each and every movement can be used to self-heal.

Principle 6: The Base – The Feet and Legs

Your feet are the hands that touch the earth. You get some gravity and energy from the earth to your whole body. If you are doing some figures on one spot, place your feet widely. You "collect" your feet together, "brush" them ONLY immediately before your next move.

You need to have a good base or platform for your balance while you lead your partner to perform some figures on the spot. Your feet are positioned on the dance floor parallel to each other with the distance of your shoulder. And mostly, the rest of the time your feet are at right angles to each other. They are never in one line. You need a Base, the foundation of all movement.

Principle 7: The Three Planes and Three Levels

Every movement can be done within three planes: low, middle and high. It can be also done in three different levels of intensity. Mixing the three levels and three planes creates a wide repertoire of movement choices.

This is what we really mean by "Improvisation": men dance the same music with different interpretation of speed and rhythm and with some of their own combinations of steps.

Principle 8: The Core of Tango: Pelvis (Tan-tien), Chest and Head. These three body weights are the home of your emotions and energy centers. The pelvis is a container of energy; you move from that point. The chest transmits and receives energy; you lead from it. Your heaviest part of the body is your head, processing the signals and energy.

Most of the time you don't move your head while dancing. When you want to direct your partner to a special step, express where she should go, you turn your head to that direction.

For example, when you want woman would go to a "Molinete" to the left, you turn your head to the left almost simultaneously with your upper body (chest) to that track. Connection to the core of the body enables you to consciously circulate and increase energy.

Principle 9: Lead by sending the energy through the channels of your arms

Your arms, hands, and fingers are extensions of your feelings and thoughts. They allow you to express yourself in personal and purposeful ways. Use them as your tools to redirect the energy, lead and create connections.

Principle 10: Trust your intuition

It is useful to practice to use your eye and other sensors and read the energy around you. Use your intuition to "see" within. You can penetrate the veil of your flesh to reveal the proper placement of your bones, tendons, ligaments and muscles and then use this information to self-heal.

Principle 11: Fitness/Tango is the Business of the Body

Any success asks for persistency and determination. If your goal is to become a good tango dancer/leader, you need to set this goal and make some plans.

When you dance, you are listening to the voices of the body. If you are not comfortable and not confident while dancing, if your partners aren't satisfied, you need to work more with your skills and attain better results. Achieving success is a process of conscious change. It is a purposeful effort to act!

Principle 12: Continuing Your Body, Mind, Spirit Education by learning Tango.

Healing the body is a practice that never ends. Every new Tango lesson is an opportunity to reeducate your body, mind and spirit.

Principle 13: Dance What You Sense

When students understand that Tango/life should be lived through sensation, only then they experience the primary lesson of it and they become connected. When they feel the precious present moment, they understand, feel and agree that dancing for enjoyment releases endorphins, improve strength, contribute to longevity.

Tango-Chi

The Argentine Tango is a passionate and intimate dance. Since the 19th century, Tango has been a dialogue between partners, a way to create living art and a dramatic form of communication through movements. The dance was born from the combinations of many cultures and their folk dances. We can see clearly, that one of the main influences came from Italian Fencing. This is how the two main positions of tango were danced: Stop or "Parada" and Cut or "Corte." We will talk more about it later. Also, we found that tango is very close to the ancient art form, TAIJI QUAN (Taichi Chuan). Similar to Tai Chi, tango focuses on developing a relationship with your smooth and slow dance, as a walking meditation. As in Tai-Chi, tango walk comes from a lower center of gravity in the body, called the "tan-tien". It is located two inches below the navel in the center of the pelvis. Learning how well you can move from this center, while walking forward as a whole block, will develop sensory awareness and a nourishing energy; some relationship between your body and the world around you.

Our special tango exercises with a balloon between the foreheads of a couple, rings on the floor and shawls in the air involve circular, elegant and soft movements, which are reminiscent of swimming in water. This fluidity gives definition to the body without the use of external weight and slowly and gently increases your range of motion.

Coordinating arm, eye and hand motions with the whole body creates graceful systematic movement without causing strain to the skeletal system.

When our students are learning to speak the Language of Tango Dance, they learn through some special exercises, steps and techniques, on how to build flexibility and strength.

***

The Bandoneon

It was invented by a German, Heinrich Band. Then, it was imported to Argentina in 1866, but not really surface until the 1870s. I can say that with the advent of the bandoneon and its entry into the Tango orchestra, the real Argentinian Tango was born. - Domingo Federico

Stages of Learning

Tango is a very intellectual and spiritual dance. Therefore, before coming to a Tango class, every person needs to prepare some available space inside his mind. Tango special exercises at the beginning of each lesson could move students through several cycles or stages of learning process. Each stage is designed to deliver specific results. While the basic moves remain the same, the students' experience changes based on how they adjust the focus, speed, intensity and overall intent.

The ability of students to remain aware and responsive to their body's ever changing needs will enable them to receive maximum benefit from each tango lesson. The Body's Way reminds us that everything in nature moves in cycles/stages to maintain harmony and balance.

In tango we see several stages of the learning process:

Stage 1: Get ready physically, mentally, emotionally and spiritually by centering and getting ready to learn a dance. Leave behind all distractions and activate your body's sensory awareness as the starting point for all action.

Stage 2: Choose a Focus and Intent. "Where is your attention placed"?

Your intent describes what you personally desire to achieve. Your focus defines where you will place your attention in order to achieve that intent. Example: "Today I will focus on the feet in order to enhance the sensation of stability in the body". For each class we provide the focus and intent, but people should also personalize it to fit their own specific needs. Stage 3: Students need to do special exercises on tango techniques, at the beginning of each class.

"Prepare Your Heart, Lungs and 13 Joints"

At the beginning of each class, students engage in some special exercises to consciously activate the flow of energy in all 13 joints, increase body heat and respiration.

These special exercises give people some awareness of how their body feels, how they adapt to the speed, intensity and range of motion, and how they work with the three planes and three levels of body movement.

Stage 4: "Cool Down - Calm, Harmonize and Re-center". Slow down to re-center, balance and harmonize the body, mind, emotions and spirit. Prepare to move on the floor. Listen to the voices of your body, telling you which muscles and joints need more attention to bring balance and harmony to your body, mind, emotions and spirit.

Stage 5: Tango is a combination of some strong, sharp, maybe even staccato steps, with some slow, legato movements. This special understanding of these combinations and contrast of it creates a special creative dance. Without such contrasting tango movement, a dancer looks like a cooked potato on the floor. Stage 6: Imagine that your feet have roots, which go deep in the earth and hold you.

You can think about your feet, also as your hands that grab the land. Gravity and the energy of your feet keep you down, pushing to the floor, feeling it. Men were thinking in advance about the dance floor or "Space Arrangement". Also, he needed to make an effort for some synchronization of his movements with his partner. Timing was crucial for the smooth dancing flow. During the dance, you carefully listen to the changing 8 beats of the music; you see better space and time. The music stimulates your body and you move with the music, improving your strength and flexibility. Take advantage of the heat and apply ability generated from the previous movement. Step forward or backwards with the help of some stretch from your hip, not from your knee. Open up your joints more fully.

Consciously recognize through body sensation, the self-healing and fitness benefits of your tango lessons. Purposefully and with intent, physically improve your body condition to improve your life.

Milonga Rules

All participants create special atmosphere of each Milonga (dance party). The perfect setting brings continual enjoyment for dancers. It happens when the environment is warm and friendly, the music is consistently delectably danceable throughout the evening and the dancers are entertained and engaged.

It is great to keep old tango traditions and the correct communication on the dance floor. Below are some guidelines we would like you to consider as you help create the atmosphere of a good Milonga.

In old time, men use a special technique to get a dance. They asked for that by doing "cabeceo" or inviting a lady by his head movement. One old friend said: "It is the man's privilege to kindly ask a woman to dance. It is the woman's prerogative to graciously accept or decline. Although it isn't the traditional form, if the woman takes the privilege to ask, then man has the prerogative to accept or decline."

In order to avoid any uncomfortable situations, we encourage upholding the tradition of using the cabeceo. The cabeceo is the non-verbal way of asking and accepting or declining a dance through eye-to-eye acknowledgement and body language. "Cabeza" means "head" in Spanish, and "cabeceo" is the castellano word that refers to eye contact and nod of the head that is used to signal the offer and acceptance of dancers at a milonga. The "cabeceo" serves a couple of purposes.

First, it minimizes public embarrassment...because it's a long walk back for a man who has just come all the way across the room and been turned down for a dance. It relieves pressure on the followers to accept dances with men they'd not dance with. But more importantly, a crowded milonga simply could not function without it. Hundreds of offers and acceptances must fly back and forth across the room each time a new tanda of music begins, and the Cabeceo is really the only practical way for everyone to quickly and efficiently find the right partner.

Both women and men can initiate an invitation with Cabeceo. If it appears someone does not want to dance with you, don't take it personally, and don't assume they will never want to dance with you in the future.

People often prefer to dance with friends, or have specific partner preferences for specific music. For this reason, milongas often feel "unfriendly" to beginners, because they don't have a circle of friends yet.

During the dance, respect yourself, your partner and the other dancers on the floor. Followers should do only what the body is comfortable doing.

Leaders should do only what the partners know how to do comfortable. As cool as it would be to do a gancho or a boleo followed by a gigantic volcada, your partner may not be in that stage of their ability to take care of themselves throughout the process. In addition, you may be disrespecting the space of surrounding dancers.

All tango teachers strongly insist and stress that each couple respect the lanes of dance. It is always more comfortable for everyone to keep two moving lanes with a center space for those who are still working on getting accustomed to flowing with the traffic. Leaders need to follow the traditional rules of the dance hall and traditions of Milonga.

Etiquette

Music will be presented in Tandas with Cortinas (3 sets with musical interludes). Clear the floor between Tandas in order to maximize partner exchanging.

Walk the lady back to her seat after the set; it is a gentlemanly thing to do. Plus, if you have done a good job, she might be in a trance or a bit confused about where she is on the floor. Use the Cabeceo or Eye Game to catch her for a dance (at 10 feet or 50 feet from her). Use the Cabeceo while dancing to make promises for later Courteous Navigation.

Dance in 2 or 3 lanes starting from the outside of the hall. Dance into the corners, rather than cutting them off. Merge into traffic by catching the eye of the on-coming leader. Neither block traffic (for long pauses), nor race around cutting off the other dancers. A collision requires both leaders to exchange apologies, at least by making eye contact and nodding.

Exercises

1. Move your head from side to side and around (5 times or more). 2. Staying on one bend in the knee leg, move/stretch your leg from the hip back and forward. 3. Move/circle your ankle around, then another one. 4. Move your upper body from side to side and around yourself, exercising your flexibility, your waist line (for the torque & dissociation which you will need to use during tango dancing). 5. Move your hips from side to side and around (for the tango torque). 6. Stretch your arms: Take your right elbow by your left hand and move to the left, wait for 5-10 seconds; then do the same for the other one. 7. Put your weight on your left leg, flex the knee, then bend it more and relax it. Then, extend your right leg to the side without any weight on it (necessary to develop for "corte" and other tango positions). While doing any moves/extension of the leg forward or backwards, keep the edge of your foot inside and on the floor, with your heel down, almost parallel to the floor (not up). Repeat 2-3 times, alternating legs.

Did you know...

In the early beginnings of Argentinian tango intimate contact between man and woman was considered taboo. Therefore, men had to practice with one another, as reputable women found it too obscene and improper invading the partner's space. Practicing with one another allowed for creating new dance moves and steps, the new art of the tango quickly developed.

LESSON 1

Authentic Tango "Box" (8 counts) –
"The First 8 Magical Basic Steps"

Men foot work: Right leg steps slightly diagonally left - back (Back Start #1-or a back corte). Left leg steps to your left side (Side Start #2) – or a side corte. Variation with Entrada: while you are doing you side step to the left and your woman goes with you of course, but with her right step.

At that moment, your right leg goes very fast to her right leg. You place it between her legs. It is possible if your weight on your left bend leg. You stay on your left bend leg. At the same time, your right leg stretched forward between women's legs.

Then, you withdraw your right leg, without moving your partner anywhere. Then, you continue to move your right leg forward and outside your partner's right side. But it should be very close to her leg (men's Parada). She goes backwards. Twist your body – tango torque (Salida step #3). Do one more step forward with your left leg (corte forward).

Body is diagonally to your partner (Step # 4). Then you put your feet together or make a cruzada (cross you left in front of your right leg) It is (Step # 5)- collect feet to position zero. Pose. Breathe. Left leg goes forward directly to your partner's left leg (Step #6 - parada), right leg steps to the right (Step # 7 –as a corte) "Tan - go closed". Feet together (Step #8).

Women foot work. Stretch your left leg forward (#1) very close to your partner left foot), move with your right leg to the right (#2), collect feet, have your weight on your right, left leg steps back diagonally (#3) crossing spine to the right; right leg steps back diagonally (#4), cross left leg over your right leg (cruzada #5), correct your hips towards your men, change weight to your left leg, move right leg diagonally back crossing your spine (#6). Left leg goes to the left side (#7) feet together (#8). The last part of Authentic Tango Box: Twist your body for a tango torque (Salida step #3 of the Box); one more step forward with your left leg (corte forward). Body is diagonally twisted to your partner. Then put your feet together or make cruzada.

Pause. Breathe. Left leg goes forward directly to your partner's left leg, right leg steps to the right. Feet together ("Tan – go closed"). It is interesting that from position "zero" and from position #5 men could lead (and they do it often) many different movements. They often lead just predictable ochos.

Men - Include Ocho (on the Step 5):

Take a long step by the right foot and around the right side of your partner, twist your hip to the right, then return and place your left foot directly in front and center. Energize your moves to reach a peak. Energize and condition some tango steps according to the beat and character of the music. For example, in the "First Eight Basic Steps", your "Back Start" is a very long, energetic and strong one, after which there could be a short pause, with a relaxation in the knee. If you skipped the "Back Start", and decided to do "The Side Start", or "The double side Start", it will be the strongest step in the basic; with the strongest energy and relaxation, with a pause after it. Next pause in the "Basic" will be only on the step number 5 (where the Cruzada – cross done by women), feet together (or one behind another, crossed) for men.

***

Sssh. Don't tell anyone this. This is a secret. Imagine telling a beginner man he has to learn to find the rhythm of the music, watch out for navigational hazards on the dance floor, develop a strategy on the spot for dealing with them choosing from a repertoire of movements he has learned, then lead the woman to move in the intended direction with the intended speed while maintaining the connection, and then... He has to follow the woman's response to his lead to determine the next move (within a millisecond, after all, this is not chess), and take responsibility for whatever goes wrong. And we wonder why there aren't enough men in tango? Yet the surviving men keep trying. It must be that the rewards of tango are greater than its obstacles. - Jay Rabe

LESSON 2

Pose "Corte"

We would like to give you several examples and specific explanations on some Tango poses. They are pretty simple and designed for beginners. They are nice to use during Milonga to make your dance more interesting and exciting.

In Tango people often dance several main positions which came from Italy: Corte and Parada. (Corte means "cut"). It came from the fencing movement involving a forward thrust to "cut" an opponent. In Tango dancing it has many variations. It is interesting to watch these positions when you learn or dance tango.

We could find it even inside the slow tango walk, which can be seen as a sequence of alternating "corte" and "parada" positions. That "Corte Pose" is good to use not only at the end of a dance, but in a sudden and sharp accent on a strong beat, by doing it fast and sharp. We want to explain one simple "Corte Pose" which may be done as a final stop at the end of the dance. It gives the dance an elegant ending.

Men start this "Corte Pose" from the position "Feet together" or from position #5 when women's legs are in the "cross" position. You have read about "Position # 5" in the previous lesson: "Tango 8 Magical Steps of the Box".

Man extends his left leg straight back, foot on the floor and leg straight. At the same time, he rotates his upper body slightly to the left, letting his partner know that he wants her to step forward with her right foot. He then shifts weight to the left leg and brings his body back so that left leg is bent and right leg is extended forward, right foot on the floor and leg straight. As he shifts weight backward his firm arm around the woman's bra line leads her to step forward with her right foot and shift weight onto that leg. Now she is in the classic "corte" or "cut" position: weight forward on bent leg and other leg extended to the rear with foot on the floor. Exciting variations include the woman wrapping forward leg around man's leg or even around his waist. Obviously he must support her strongly in either of these variations. To end the pose, shift weight back to the starting position, then continue forward left, side right, and close to the side—steps 6, 7, and 8 of the "Magic Eight" box. Keep your right arm on her "Bra line" and use it to direct her movements where you want her go. Enjoy the moment.

LESSON 3

Pose "Punta de Pie"

Man extends his left leg to the left and changes weight, (Side Start # 2 – side corte to the left), and before the woman can bring her feet together, he moves his right foot in a small "entrada" between her feet.

Woman steps with the man, and closes her legs collecting them together, but without changing her weight (her weight is on her right leg and she would change her weight only with her man by Tango rules).

Man's weight is still on the left foot, with his right foot between (and touching) the woman's feet. He lowers his body directly down, bending his left knee, and slowly extends his right leg to the right; carefully pushing the woman's left leg to the side. Then, they slightly arc over and look at their pointing feet. Their arms are creating a ½ circle above their heads.

They are frozen for 3 seconds in this pose - Punta De Pie.

Then, the woman brings his right leg back to the standing position. Bodies are very stable and strong, with no sideways movements. Only legs are moving out and no weight is placed on the moving legs. Then, the man takes the same right leg across his standing left leg, doing embellishments "beso" or short kiss across his left leg. Then he moves this right leg (SALIDA) forward outside his partner to Resolution, and to "Tan-go closed" (the last part of BOX). Enjoy the moment.

The leader learns tango skills knowing that he needs to focus on the follower with his heart, as the Golden Age dancers would refer to this as maintaining the relationship between the two bodies – "manteniendo la relacion entre los dos cuerpos".

***

The soul is not really united unless all the bodily energies, all the limbs of the body, are united. - Martin Buber

***

Tango is a dance in which is it easy to become obsessed with perfection. The taste of heaven that is found within tango may encourage some to seek perfection. Others may bring their own perfectionism to tango. But we should never confuse heaven and perfection. They are very different. The path of perfectionism often leads away from heaven — as we find ourselves accompanied and driven forward by demons that become all too familiar. If we pursue perfection in our practice, we are likely developing the demons that seek to keep us from effective dancing. In tango, heaven is found through the simple gift of grace. That comes from getting out on the dance floor with the person that happens to be right for the moment, opening one's heart and falling in love again. The times that this happens, one is just happy to be in the arms of another at the end of the tanda. - Stephen Brown

LESSON 4

Ochos

The name "ocho" comes from the early days of tango, when women while doing it would trace figure eight into the dirt floor. We ask our students to go to a beach and try to dance it on the sand. It is the best practice for the beginners to improve their techniques.

The ocho is the main tango step. Also, it is one of the best transitional lead/step for some interesting improvisations. It could be lead with a pivot or without it. The pivots in tango make dancers look more elegant. Most of the beginners could make follower dance ocho several times in a raw. But for an advanced follower to do it more than twice is not very interesting. So, ocho is better to use as a transitional step. Tango is a dance where men play with women's legs or between them, and a woman flirts with a man providing him that space and her legs. Before we will dance a pivoted ocho, it is good for a follow to know something important hints to make a dance as a fun.

Suggestions: In most steps, a woman needs to provide a long leg to a leader, a leg with an extension. Then, smart leader use the chance to play with it. The more you relaxed and receptive to a leader, the better you could feel the right lead for an ocho. Follower shoulders and chest should mirror or stay in front of the leader when he leads woman into a pivot. It is good if your hips move naturally, following the shoulders. It is good to add some muscle power for a better pivot. Followers always mirror the amount of energy that leader give them. When you take a back step (straight behind crossing your own spine), always first reach the floor with your foot, and then transfer your weight on it. While moving, between the steps, bring your feet together very fast, as your brash them. Followers, as well as leaders, should maintain your own balance and axis throughout the ocho. It could be achieved when your ribs up, shoulders down, and the most important, your bone tail is vertically to the floor (not in a diagonal position). So, watch your bone tail and you will be balanced.

Men foot work: Trampa (triple steps) is the easiest way to lead lady to an ocho. Trampa: one big step, one short (feet together), one big. It could be done forward or to the side. Side start to the left (as a trampa - trap). Then, he brings his right leg to his left, and immediately does another side start. At the same time, he is leading his partner by his shoulders and upper body slightly moving to the left, helping his woman by his arm. For the ocho it might be very important to open slightly your embrace and allow follower to do her pivot more comfortable. When men move forward with these steps, it is good to cares (brush) one foot over the other (closing faster his feet before the next step). Also, men need to step around the women, when they do progressing forward ocho and moving in the dance floor (advanced dancers).

Women foot work: Follow your man to the side step. Stop the movements in the middle of his chest, but don't go too far to his left side. Then follower pivots on her right leg, and at the same time, she moves her left leg back (straight line crossing the spine) behind her and step. Put your feet together, collect or brush between the movements. Then pivot on the left leg, put feet together (or brash), and right foot back.

Front Ocho

It is done in the same way, except it uses forward steps rather than back steps. It often led from the cross (when a woman/ man is in crusada - Step #5). It could be done from other steps. So, followers should be always ready to pivot and not to miss the lead. Followers move the shoulders and chest in a way that they mimic the leader, just as in the pivoted back ocho. Extend your foot forward; transfer your weight to it. In order to be in a harmony with your leader, listen carefully to his energy and determine what size, or how long your step should be. Collect your feet together and be always ready for a potential pivot into another ocho. Always be ready to do a pivot, to be flexible and understanding of your leader. When you keep your shoulders facing the leader you will create a stronger spiral, which helps your hips do a natural pivot. Depending on your flexibility, a back ocho may move against the line of the dance and cause the leader to step backwards. Remember that an ocho is done with a cross step rather than an open step.

Benefits of Dancing

Have the best time of your life!

Dance is a great emotional healer. The music alone can help soothe, excite or inspire you. Once you begin moving to the music you'll start to release tension and stress, your focus will be drawn away from your problems, and if you allow yourself to become absorbed in the experience, you will smile, laugh and really enjoy it.

Dancing could act as an escape from the real world and be a very personal, therapeutic activity. Some styles of dance allow you to express your thoughts and feelings through movement. If you don't want to talk or write about your feelings, dance them.

Movements can be used to tell a story, redirect and exert negative, positive and emotional energy, share feelings, calm and relax you, or excite and inspire you. For those looking to break some barriers, dance is a great way to find and get to know other people. It is also a great way to find and get to know yourself. How? By involving yourself in the world of dance can help you grow as a person physically, emotionally, mentally and socially.

Dancing tests your body in many ways: coordination, strength, stamina, balance, stress response, and response to relaxation. Over time, you will learn a lot about how your body responds to different exercises and situations and you will learn how to train and condition your body to react certain ways. You'll also become very familiar with your body's natural limitations.

You can push yourself, but it is very important to respect these limitations and take care of your body. Dance can also be used to help break mental and emotional barriers. Chances are that those "barriers" are also reflected in other areas of life. If you focus on breaking your "dance barriers", once you succeed, you will have broken barriers in many other parts of your life. Some say that the best way to overcome your fears is to face them, so why not use something fun like dance to make those mental/emotional breakthroughs.

Social growth occurs naturally...the more involved you get with dance or any activity for that matter, the more people you meet and befriend. The unique thing about dance is that it is very often done with a partner. Certain styles of dance are meant for two (like tango)!

The nice thing about dancing with a partner is that you learn to communicate and compromise. You can't just focus on or worry about yourself, you have to be aware of your partner, and potentially other couples around you. Both partners are responsible for meshing their skills and communicating in order to have a nice, enjoyable dance together.

In addition, you learn a lot about other people, like, it's really not so bad to ask somebody to dance or smile and laugh with them, and, it's fun to dance with people who have different styles. The best part is all the fun of the social dancing atmosphere whether you're looking to meet new people or expand your social etiquette, dance and dance and dance.

In talking about the health benefits of tango dance, Elena said, "When students dance the tango, they relax, lose weight, improve strength, and increase longevity.

Additional benefits are even more immediate. "Tango might make people feel sexier and less depressed."

Elena encourages couples to get involved in Tango "as a weekly date night with a purpose".

Research confirms that authentic Argentine Tango dance lessons helps heal neurological disorders such as Parkinson's disease, improving both physical and neurological health, and increase testosterone levels.

Elena says that she sees Tango dance lessons as a form of couple's therapy, enhancing the relationship through subtle physical, spiritual and emotional communication between partners, which tango gives.

Tango brings more appreciation for life and deep awareness for the present moment. It teaches how to listen to each other, how to be patient and stable.

Tango helps followers to learn how to be quiet, to have deeper sensitivity and ability to surrender. It is a healer, an escape, a source of encouragement, an act of happiness. Every person will get something different out of their experience, and have that to grow on and share with others. Leaders learn how to be active thinker, fast, artistic, resourceful creator and initiator.

Tango makes life more inspiring and meaningful. It fills every day with more joy and energy, and brings more stimulation. It helps to develop more control over life and balance it. Tango is the most challenging concentration of the mind. But it gives you a lot of pleasure and fun when you advanced it to the Freedom of Creativity and Artistic Power (a great task for some strong personalities).

***

Learning Authentic Tango

Strange acrobatics of a human ball curled up in a strange dance, provocative and artistic, which does not admit any reference or comparison to any other dance of all time and of all peoples. - Vicente Rossi (1926).

**

That Martin Buber and the early Jewish mystics said more about the nature of the tango than modern dance critics. At the beginning it was an orgiastic mischief, today it is a way of walking. I learned that this most physically active and demanding of the arts is essentially about stillness. That music is, at its core, a way of describing silence. That performing is more about the invisible inside than the visible outside. That pleasure - taken to its extremity - becomes work. And work - taken to its extremity - becomes love. That is how I started out trying to make a film about the joy of dance and ended up making a story about the complexity of love,-- "The Tango Lesson", Film by Sally Potter.

"Ask And You Shall be Given"

I asked God for water, and I got an ocean. I asked God for a flower, and I got a garden. I asked God for a tree, and I got a forest. I asked God for a friend, and I got you and Tango...There is not enough darkness in the world to put out the light of my candle: the Candle of Love, Hope and Friendship. And my candle loses nothing by lighting another candle...

***

In 2004 Elena and Victor Pankey formed Tango Caminito School, a nonprofit international dance company based in Fallbrook, California. They feel very strongly about their endeavor. The main idea of Tango Caminito School was to teach people how to dance with joy. The most valuable was to help benefit people's health and wellbeing, increase the closeness shared by couple during the dance, and to broaden people's social exposure. Dressed in colorful Tango-style dress, with great music, and fascinating comments about dance, Elena and Victor, set a festive tone and deliver an authentic Argentine Tango dance experience.

In the tango classes, the melodic strains and syncopated rhythms of Tango music fill the air. The dance studio is dressed up with long colorful curtains, along with paintings and photos of tango dancers. "Students step here into an atmosphere of a Caminito Street in Buenos Aires,"- Elena said.

Victor provides colorful historical background during the lessons and explains how Tango evolved in the late 1800s.

The Founders said that the private lessons are the most effective approach to fast progress in the Tango life. They feel that some special people with fire in their hearts, with dreams in their eyes, with love for this life, will always learn tango faster.

Enicia, a tango student, says, "We have been taking private lessons from Victor and Elena. They are true artists and we're thrilled they have been offering their gifts to people."

"Authentic Arg. Tango differs from American or Ballroom style Tango," Elena said.

Tango is like traveling: the more you know about it, the more it tells you, that you are at the beginning of your road. Moreover, dancing tango is like writing a book: nobody can hide his or her personality while doing it. When we read something, we see the vocabulary and usage of the words, the style and structure of the paragraphs. We see the author character behind the description of the subject. The same happens in tango.

There are many different styles in tango, different teaching techniques. When a teacher has good knowledge and a clear understanding of tango history, development, dance techniques, that teacher should have very pleasant and clearly structured lessons. As someone once said, that with a clear thinking comes clear teaching.

Dancing and learning tango has different meanings and purposes for different people. People come to learn tango because they were motivated by the incredible images, tango movies, by the beauty of the music, or by an atmosphere of romance and nostalgia. Sometimes, with apologies to Shakespeare, Elena said: "Tango is life. Life is a theater. Tango is a theater of your life."

Learning Authentic Tango

Since tango is a relationship therapy, it is good to teach couples with established communication and help them to improve it.

Some students wrote: "Hi Elena! We are Chinese. But I've loved to listen and dance Tango since I was 10. You again reopened for me, a new world of tango. Your instructions are very clear and easy for us to learn! We appreciate your work. Thanks for your excellent teaching technique." Alice and Alan, Orange County, California.

During dance lessons students learn history, development of the dances, meaning of some tango steps, influence of dances on each other, differences, similarities between them. They learn characteristic of tango, vocabulary, music, the value of silent connection, balance, and stability.

Tango never ends, nor does the process of learning it. It does not matter whether you are a teacher or an advanced dancer, you just go from one level to another, practicing and dancing tango together, they have a way to a better, longer, and more beautiful life!

Elena and Victor also continue to grow in tango. They travel to Argentina frequently to advance their teaching skills under some of the best Tango Masters in the world. If people listen to each other during the dance, they will learn more about each other. Ladies, even some who like to control, are looking for a confident man, a leader. They don't like men who doubt, either in life or in tango. If the gentleman understands where he is going, if he is not confused with his own decisions, ladies will enjoy dancing with him.

Learning Authentic Tango

One of Elena's 97 years old students, Eddy Lange, from La Jolla, who began to learn to dance in Vienna, in the forties, wrote: "Elena, you are teaching with such joy and enthusiasm! It is a joy to be in your class. I am telling you that because I also see that you both are tremendous business people. But I love your way of teaching that is why I come. Thank you."

Elena said that the passion for Tango is the hidden, unconscious desire for eternity. People enjoy learning tango. When they feel the music, and deeply understand the powerful present moment of our life. It is the best to start learning this dance from the classical Tango Salon, where students could get all tools they need for it, and for attending, enjoying social tango dancing party, Milonga. From its first day of establishment in 2004 to the present time, Tango Caminito School has been actively participating in community and charity work for the benefits of society. Elena thrilled to produce with great success many different shows, and the proceeds from it often go to a charity. Tango Caminito Company and their students for many years have enjoyed performing at a variety of great venues in California. The shows present variations of ethnic dances from around the world. Elena also offers interesting historical anecdotal information for people who wish to learn more, and explains how authentic Argentine Tango evolved in the 19 century, the cultural nuances and the fit with both costuming and music.

Elena Pankey is the Founder and Artistic Director of the Tango Caminito School. She is a Certified Tango Argentine Dance Instructor with "Tango Educator" Diploma. Elena is a Tango Master, and dances it as a

Learning Authentic Tango

leader and a follower. Elena is also teaching Ballroom, Latin, Ruska/Roma (Russian Gypsy) dance lessons.

Elena finished prestigious Leningrad State University as the philologist-linguist, was teaching literature in Russian schools. She has about 45 years of job experience in different areas of art education, literature, music, dance Theater. She worked as an assistant producer in Russian cinematography, sound assistant of the movie productions, Radio journalist, and newspaper correspondent. She owned her own businesses and traveled the world.

After fifteen years of teaching Argentine Tango, Elena designed a special original tango course which helps people to improve the quality of lives and marriages. It is great to learn Authentic Tango Argentine style as a Couple's Dance Therapy. Elena is using ancient Auroveda wisdom while teaching tango, reminding that visualization is the key to mastering The Law of Attraction, where everyone's wish comes true.

Owners of Russian Musical Theater in San Diego, Zin and Aida once said:

"Elena! You were magnificent last night at the Russian Theater dancing improvisational Tango. You are the best performer in San Diego. Moreover, you would be an exceptional performer even in Buenos Aires, and we have seen several their high profile shows. Your technical skills are just an addition to your look, appearance, your expression of Tango music. It would be an honor for me to crown you as a Tango Queen of San Diego. BRAVO

Terminology

For good dancers it is important to learn more about the tango music and orchestras. **Essential Tango Orchestras:** Lucia DeMare, Rudolfo Biagi, Enrique Rodriguez, Francini Pontier, Osvaldo Fresedo, Jose Baso, Hector Varela, Mariano Mores, Los Tubatango, Francisco Lomuto, Julio DeCaro, Edgardo Donato, Florindo Sassone, Alfredo Gobbi, Leopoldo Federeco, Donato Racciatti, Roberto Firpo, Horacio Salgan. **Ten Big Orchestras:** Osvaldo Pugliese, Carlos DiSarli, Juan D'Arienzo, Miguel Calo, Francisco Canaro, Ricardo Tanturi, Anibal Troilo, D Agostino/Vargas, Pedro Laurenz, Alfredo DeAngelis

Contemporary: Astor Piazzolla

***

AMAGUE (from amagar): an embellishment either led or done on one's own to the other foot. ABRIR: to open. BARRIDA or SWEEP: Sweeping motion. A leg push; one partner's foot sweeps the other's foot along the floor. Also, it called llevada. BOLEODORES: a rope with weighted balls at either end used by gauchos. CADENA: chain. CADENCIA or RHYTHM: Any steps done in a rhythm of syncopation. CAMINAR: To walk; important part of Argentine tango dancing. CANYENGUE: an older style of tango. El COMPAS: the beat. CALESITA: The lead steps in a circle around the follower - keeping them on their own axis. CORTINA curtain [cor-tee-nah] - A musical interlude following a tanda at a milonga. MOREPASO

BASICO or COMMON BASIC: The base of many tango patterns. CRUZAR (Crusada): to cross. DIBUJO or TRACE: To trace your partner's foot. ESCUCHAR: to listen. FIJARSE: or pay close attention. ENGANCHE or HOOKING/COUPLING: Occurs when lead wraps a leg around their partner's leg. Leader displaces follower's feet from inside. ENROSQUE (from enroscar): To coil or twist. While tango used for performance. GANCHO or HOOK: To hook. A quick motion of the leg bending at the knee, catching partner's leg. GIRO or TURN: While partner does a molinete the lead turns on one foot placing the toe of the other foot in front and executing a sharp turn. GUIAR: to lead. IZQUIERDA: left. LLEVAR: to lead or to carry. LLEVADA (from llevar): To transport. (See barridas). LAPIZ: a circular figure drawn with foot. MEDIA VUELTA: half turn. LA MARCA: the lead. MOLINETE or CIRCLING: Forward and back ochos (figure 8-s. MORDIDA (bite) or SANDWICH: One partner's foot is sandwiched between the other partner's foot. OCHOS or EIGHTS: Figure 8-s (similar to fans done in other Latin dances). OPEN/CLOSE: Refers to the arms and hands while in dance position. The open position is the lead's left hand and the follower's right hand. The closed position is the lead's left arm and hand and the follower's right arm and hand. PARADA or STOP: To move and stop a partner's foot by pushing their foot with your own. POCKET: Anytime the lead walks on outside of partner - either hip.. RESOLUCION or RESOLUTION: Ending of a common basic. SACADA or REMOVE, WITHDRAW: To displace - to move your partner's foot with your own. SALIDA or EXIT: To begin. SALIDA CRUZADA: The first half of a common basic. SALUDO: Front leg wipe. SALON: Style of tango best suited for social dancing. Always following line of dance, being aware and courteous to others. SECOND: Open position or side step. Body is balanced over open feet. SENTADA or SIT POSITION: A sitting action. Weight on one leg with bent knee; other leg out straight, with knees together. SYNCOPATION: To modify rhythm by a shift of accents on a beat. TRABADA or TRAPPED: To lock.

***

The best book for everybody about Tango is "**Master Manipulations**". You will learn how Tango influences, shapes, and impacts the lives and relationships of those who dance it. Furthermore, this book will give you a great insight into the psychology and history of tango, as well as on the communication and forces that revolve around this living dance. It has it all. Get it now for your fun life and dancing! It has it all.

***

The tango is a direct expression of something that poets have often tried to state in words: the belief that a fight may be a celebration. - Jorge Luis Borges, 1950.

***

More: www.TangoCaminito.com
Enjoy our video channel:
http://www.youtube.com/TangoCaminito

Epilogue

Learning essential Argentine tango leading and following techniques will bring you to a powerful dance - life. Learning this dance will increase your balance, concentration, and mental power. It is an essential book for men and women, beginners and advanced dancers. This book teaches people how to be in control of their own dance and life, while influencing and empowering your partner. It is the most useful and easy reading book for any person who wants to learn Argentine tango faster and dance confidently. This book is for men, women, beginners, and advanced dancers. It teaches how to influence and empower your partner. It is useful book to know about how leaders should lead their tango well and be successful. Also, it is about how to become a beautiful follower to give men the best time ever. This book has unique information about the dance, which is always in demand. People often cannot find it anywhere else.

This book helps to solve some problem that many people have, while they are learning to dance. Ever wondered what's the meaning behind the intricate leg movements of the tango dancers? Or what are the authentic dance patterns of the Tango? Or what's the secret behind the sensual way the woman follows the man on the tango dance floor? Or what are the etiquette and courtesy during a Milonga?

If your response to any of these questions is yes, the chapters for leaders will help you delve deeper into all these answers. If you have question how to make man happier and keep him around you with his smile on the face, then learn how to follow him well.

This book contains it all: the Tango principles, stages of learning, key body positions and patterns of leading. The stories in this book are compelling and entertaining, as well as Elena Pankey, the author, who was a celebrity of 70-80th in Russian theater and cinematography. While reading this book you learn all about the leading technique and following, while improving your dance style, and becoming a stronger leader or a beautiful follower in your dance or in your real life. Immerse into Tango-Dance adventure to discover principals of Golden Age Tango Techniques. Investigate how to listen to each other, relax and improve your partnerships. Learn authentic tango movements, experiment how to be more balanced, focused, how to get positive energy. Improve your ability to read another person's mind without verbal communication. Enjoy active dance workout, meet and make new friends. Learn new culture, open up your horizon. Enjoy our unique Tango dance lessons for any age, level of dancing, shapes, or social status.

51312914R00062

Made in the USA
San Bernardino, CA
19 July 2017